NEW KIDS ON THE BLOCK · STOP IT GIRL · DID (BLOW YOUR MIND)
POPSICLE · ANGEL · BE MY GIRL · NEW KIDS ON THE
WANNA BE LOVED BY YOU · DON'T GIVE UP ON ME ·
TOUGH · YOU GOT IT (THE RIGHT STUFF) · PLEASE DON'T GO GIRL · I'LL
BE LOVING YOU (FOREVER) · COVER GIRL · I NEED YOU · HANGIN' TOUGH
REMEMBER WHEN · WHAT'CHA GONNA DO (ABOUT IT) · MY FAVORITE GIRL
HOLD ON · MERRY, MERRY CHRISTMAS · THIS ONE'S FOR THE CHILDREN · LAST
NIGHT I SAW SANTA CLAUS · I'LL BE MISSING YOU COME CHRISTMAS (A LETTER
TO SANTA) · I STILL BELIEVE IN SANTA CLAUS · MERRY, MERRY CHRISTMAS
THE CHRISTMAS SONG · FUNKY, FUNKY XMAS · WHITE CHRISTMAS · THE LITTLE
DRUMMER BOY · THIS ONE'S FOR THE CHILDREN · STEP BY STEP · TONIGHT · BABY, I
BELIEVE IN YOU · CALL IT WHAT YOU WANT · LET'S TRY IT AGAIN · HAPPY BIRTHDAY
GAMES · TIME IS ON OUR SIDE · WHERE DO I GO FROM HERE? · STAY WITH ME
BABY · FUNNY FEELING · NEVER GONNA FALL IN LOVE AGAIN · FACE THE MUSIC
YOU GOT THE FLAVOR · DIRTY DAWG · GIRLS · IF YOU GO AWAY · KEEP ON SMILIN'
NEVER LET YOU GO · KEEPIN' MY FINGERS CROSSED · MRS. RIGHT · SINCE
YOU WALKED INTO MY LIFE · LET'S PLAY HOUSE · I CAN'T BELIEVE IT'S OVER
'LL STILL BE LOVING YOU · I'LL BE WAITIN' · THE BLOCK · CLICK CLICK CLICK
SINGLE · BIG GIRL NOW · SUMMERTIME · 2 IN THE MORNING · GROWN MAN
DIRTY DANCING · SEXIFY MY LOVE · TWISTED · FULL SERVICE · LIGHTS,
CAMERA, ACTION · PUT IT ON MY TAB · STARE AT YOU · 10 · WE OWN TONIGHT
REMIX (I LIKE THE) · TAKE MY BREATH AWAY · WASTED ON YOU · FIGHTING
GRAVITY · MISS YOU MORE · THE WHISPER · JEALOUS (BLUE) · CRASH
BACK TO LIFE · NOW OR NEVER · SURVIVE YOU · LET'S GO OUT WITH A BANG

NEW KIDS ON THE BLOCK

40TH ANNIVERSARY CELEBRATION

NEW KIDS ON THE BLOCK

40TH ANNIVERSARY CELEBRATION

Selena Fragassi

EPIC INK

The New Kids On The Block, left to right:
Donnie Wahlberg, Jordan Knight, Joey McIntyre,
Jonathan Knight, and Danny Wood.

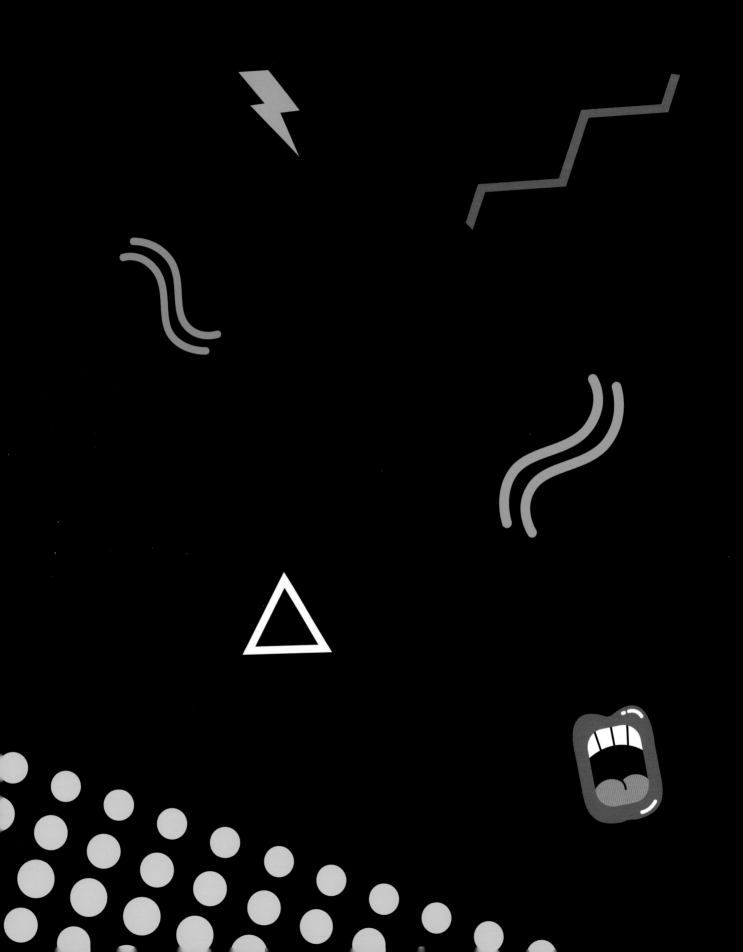

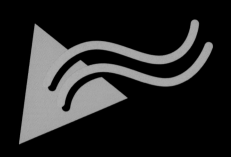

**FOR MY #1 FANS,
MY FAMILY**

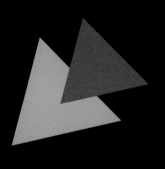
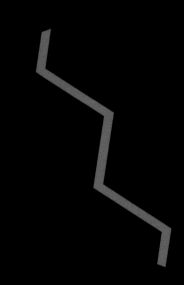

CONTENTS

NKOTB performs at TD Garden in Boston in June 2019.

NKOTB performs in
London in 2012.

Something in the stars aligned for New Kids On The Block in 1984, when five humble kids from Boston came together and went on to become both one of the biggest pop groups in the world and the model upon which future boy bands were molded. For all intents and purposes, Donnie, Danny, Jordan, Jonathan, and Joey weren't poised to be megastars who sold 80 million albums, crossed the $1 billion threshold for merchandise, had the highest-grossing tour in 1991, and have continued their career for 40-plus years while other pop groups of their ilk packed up and called it a day.

These were five kids from inner-city Boston who happened to be in the right place at the right time in the right era. Their eventual producer was a man named Maurice Starr, who was simply looking for his next New Edition after being embarrassingly fired by that group for money mismanagement. His grassroots talent search brought him to one Donnie Wahlberg, who recommended some schoolyard friends.

New Kids On The Block built a career on being wholesome role models for kids caught in the crosshairs of adults shrouding the youth from drug wars, the AIDS epidemic, and the "devil's music"—heavy metal. But perhaps the most wholesome part of all was a band so rooted in friendship they also set a model for how to be good coexisting humans. It's an MO that extends into their devout fanbase, lovingly self-identified as Blockheads, who have clung to the group like they're extended family. Fans constantly buy out shows, cruises, and conventions, and have helped return the modern NKOTB to the stadiums they played in their heyday.

In their prime, New Kids On The Block (first called Nynuk) were the epitome of their own "Hangin' Tough" motto. Their debut album in 1986 was an abominable failure and they were *this close* to being yanked from the Columbia Records roster and becoming a distant memory only to the people living in Boston who saw them playing at local fairs, dances, and retirement homes. But they stuck it out and soon found fame.

Maurice had a marketing vision to try to sell "white kids with soul" to Black consumers and it grossly backfired—that is, until the kids took the stage for "Amateur Night" at the famed Apollo Theatre in Harlem one October night in 1988 and enjoyed a standing ovation. Their crossover appeal became apparent, and their close relationships with Black artists have been a hallmark of their career in the decades since. Four of the five members of New Kids On The Block hailed from Dorchester (all but Joey, who was much younger and from a different neighborhood) and were bussed to schools in Roxbury as part of Boston's controversial pilot program to desegregate public schools. It's here they got a crash course in hip-hop, soul, R&B, street culture, and breakdancing.

As much as NKOTB fans can claim New Kids as the nostalgic music of their youth, acts like Michael Jackson, Public Enemy, and even New Edition were the cornerstone of the cultural coming-of-age for the "Step By Step" hitmakers. In future years, they'd continue to tap into this first love, dabbling in rap and hip-hop in their material and finding collaborations with the likes of Salt-N-Pepa, Naughty By Nature, Boyz II Men, and Bell Biv DeVoe.

New Kids On The Block have survived lip-syncing scandals, grueling two-year-straight tour schedules, their personal lives becoming tabloid fodder (or, in the case of Jonathan, being kept a total secret for many years), and uncertainty as the music landscapes changed in the early '90s and their fanbase simply "grew up." But still, they stayed by, "hangin' tough" and being their authentic selves. In the interim years, they embarked on a litany of solo projects, from albums to Broadway to Hollywood, to a smorgasbord of reality TV shows. They were awarded a star on the Hollywood Walk of Fame and their own holiday (celebrated April 24 every year), and have played their beloved Fenway Park in Boston three times. They never went quietly into the night; there was still music to make.

When they announced their comeback in 2008 in an appearance on *The Today Show*, throngs of people stood in the pouring rain and cold to be part of the reunion for which they had waited so long. And ever since, New Kids On The Block have found ways to "keep up" with the times and reinvent rather than remain a shell of a bygone era.

Incredibly, their post-reunion second coming has been active longer than the first go-around and shows no signs of slowing. As Arsenio Hall said in the band's Hollywood Walk of Fame ceremony, "These songs will be our oldies when we are old. We have the greatest oldies in the history of music because we have New Kids."

The New Kids photographed in Los Angeles in 1989.

STEP BY STEP

New Kids On The Block perform
"Please Don't Go Girl" on *Soul Train* in 1988

"Consider the family tree that this man is the very root and foundation of. Start with New Edition and New Kids On The Block and go on from there. Consider the artists, the actors, the producers, the television shows, the music, the movies, and the talent that were born of those two bands. Then imagine the vacuum that would be left behind were it not for us having Maurice Starr and his amazing gift."

—Donnie on Instagram, 2019

The New Kids in Orlando in 1989.

CHAPTER ONE

MAKING THE BAND

A good leader can take a band from invisible to recognized. A great producer can help steer a career and break records. An even better manager walks away when it's time to do so. Maurice Starr held every one of these identities at one point or another in the career of New Kids On The Block, the group he hand-assembled and brought to the precipice of infamy beginning in the 1980s.

Without his influence, we may have never known Donnie, Danny, Jonathan, Jordan, and Joey, let alone seen them perform together over the past 40 years. Though his name might not be as recognizable as those of the Fab Five, there would be no story to tell without the character of Maurice Starr.

Born Larry Curtis Johnson and raised in Deland, Florida, Maurice was first encouraged to find his way in the music industry by his professional trumpet-playing father (who once worked with Ray Charles). After uprooting and moving to Boston in the 1970s, Maurice was initially part of a musical brotherhood himself, the hip-hop funk troupe made up of his siblings, the Jonzun Crew. After leaving the band and trying (and failing at) a solo career, Maurice decided to instead find music acts that could perform the songs he wrote to greater mass appeal. Over time, he became the great and powerful music Oz behind sales of 50 million albums and effectively created *the* model for all the boy bands of the future. Although, New Kids On The Block is actually not the first act he managed.

Maurice's official Instagram page lists him as an "award winning hit producer, songwriter,

week—an interesting fact, since New Edition was really just Maurice's attempt at making the "new edition" of one the true OG boy bands, the Jackson 5. *Candy Girl* would go on to sell 1 million copies, supported by New Edition's tour dates where Madonna even opened for them at one stop at New York's Roseland Ballroom. But when the band arrived back home to Boston and each member reportedly only received a paycheck of $1.87, Maurice was accused of embezzlement, fired on the spot, and was on to his next project.

Much like he had done in the early days, Maurice embarked on a new talent search—except this time he had his eye on creating a pop/R&B group made up of white teenagers. "If New Edition was as big as they were, I could imagine what would happen if white kids were doing the same thing," he told the *New York Times* in 1990.

"[Maurice] started telling people his next group would be a new Osmond Brothers—white kids who could go over big in Black neighborhoods—and that they'd be stars. People thought he was nuts," says *Boston.com*.

Initially, Maurice "took it to the streets" to find his protégés, as he told *MusiquePlus* in 1990, recounting a story of guerilla tactics that once involved giving his business card to a kid he heard singing in a flower shop. Except, instead of hearing back from the talented young star or his family, Maurice got a call from the FBI, wondering why he was giving out his number to young children.

That tactic was soon aborted and Maurice called on his friend and business partner, Mary Alford, to help. As Maurice told *Entertainment Weekly* in 1990, he didn't trust his own judgment, saying, "I think I can make anybody a star." On the other hand, Mary "knew a lot of

and music mogul," which is a reputation he had built by the year 1984, when he started a talent search in the greater Boston area for his next big act.

At the time, he had just worked his magic with another Boston-bred group, New Edition, the early project of Bobby Brown as well as Ricky Bell, Michael Bivins, and Ronnie DeVoe (the latter three who would go on to form Bell Biv DeVoe). Maurice discovered that group in 1981 after hosting his Hollywood Talent Nights at Boston's Strand Theatre. He then helped write and produce the teenage R&B act's debut album, *Candy Girl*, in 1983, which was led by the blockbuster title track.

In May of that year, *Candy Girl* notably hit the number one spot on the *Billboard Hot R&B/Hip-Hop Songs* chart (formerly known as the *Hot Black Singles* chart), besting even "Beat It" by the King of Pop, Michael Jackson, for a

neighborhoods for white playground break dancers, rappers, and singers."

At first, Mary provided a list of about 50 potential stars. Maurice's criteria? As he told *MusiquePlus*, they had to have a "nice look, a nice personality . . . hip-hop and soul, and know how to rap and break dance."

It was fifteen-year-old Donnie Wahlberg who was the first member chosen (along with his thirteen-year-old brother Mark Wahlberg, a short-lived member). As such, Donnie became the natural-born leader of the group. According to Maurice, Donnie was spontaneous: "He could rap and never stop." When prompted, Donnie came up with a rap about Maurice on the spot that won the manager over.

ABOVE: New Edition performs in Wisconsin in 1988.

INSET: The cover of New Edition's single "Cool It Now," released in 1984.

white kids with soul" and Maurice entrusted her with finding a talent pool they could pull from to create what would eventually become New Kids On The Block. According to a *People* cover story in 1990, Mary was asked to "scour the city's racially mixed inner-city

Once Donnie signed on the dotted line, he then suggested a group of his teenage friends from school who might be interested in the gig. His friend Jamie Kelly was recruited, though his tenure wasn't very long. Another of Donnie's friends, sixteen-year-old Jonathan Knight, was up next. He was appealing because he was sensitive (a trait Maurice thought young girls would cling to), as well as caring, which the manager believed would translate to a real sense of caring about the fans. Jonathan's brother, fourteen-year-old Jordan Knight, was another natural add-on—he was also shy but had an appealing range to his vocals that Maurice figured could add a Motown vibe to the group. Not only that, but Jordan was eager and quick to learn, taking on guitar, piano, and bass parts as well, which made him adaptable for how Maurice needed to utilize him in the group.

Similar to that rationale, Donnie's other teenage buddy, Danny Wood, was eyed for his great interest in learning all about the inner workings of a studio; even at fifteen years old, he could work a mixing board. Plus, he could breakdance and was a hard worker, always giving 150%, as Maurice recalled. Danny kept the rest of the band motivated.

Joey McIntyre was the last one to join the group, months later, upon Jamie Kelly's exit. He was another Mary find and became the baby of the group at just twelve years old. But Joey had the perfect look, according to Maurice—and when the pre-teen belted out a few notes, the manager knew his early falsetto range would be the perfect accompaniment. In fact, Maurice sent Joey home with a Michael Jackson tape to study, so he could better understand how to tap into his upper vocal range. After poring over the material, Joey returned to the studio and laid down vocals for the early NKOTB song, "Please Don't Go Girl." Maurice recalled, "Everyone thought he was Michael Jackson."

Though it's been said Joey didn't exactly fit in with the group at first and was often pranked by his older bandmates, he persevered and became an indelible member. And with that, the New Kids were formed.

"That's the part of New Kids history I don't think most people get. They think it's some big competition where 1,000 boys tried out. It wasn't that, it was so grassroots," Donnie told *PopStruck* in 2019.

Maurice originally named the group with the nonsense moniker Nynuk. No one really knows where the name came from (it could've been the 1922 movie *Nanook of the North*, or the name of the dog in *Lost Boys,* or even the nonsense saying that the Three Stooges used to utter). Maurice began coaching the teens in the studio and in rehearsals, where they learned choreography and showmanship. Maurice was also the one who wrote all of the band's big early hits (just like he once did for New Edition), including every track on their breakthrough album, *Hangin' Tough*, which birthed the title track, as well as "You Got It (The Right Stuff)" and "I'll Be Loving You (Forever)," among others.

In the beginning, Maurice booked his budding quintet anywhere he could—from high school dances to retirement homes—and though there were many trials and tribulations along the way (including the band cutting ties with Maurice ahead of the release of *Face The Music* in 1994), those early efforts paid off: New Kids On The Block became one of the biggest bands of all time, with over 80 million albums sold.

Maurice's great influence is one that the members themselves have not forgotten all

WHO WAS THE FIRST BOY BAND?

According to *Rolling Stone*, New Kids On The Block "set the template for the boy bands of the late 1990s." While it's true they were the predecessor for NSYNC, Backstreet Boys, 98 Degrees, and countless others to come after, who paved the way for them? If you ask Danny Wood, he believes the originators of the first boy bands are the Jackson 5, the Osmonds, and New Edition. Some have argued the origins go back even farther, to the Monkees and the debut of their show in 1966 (though others say that their Beatles-spoof origins don't qualify).

No matter where you stand, here's a timeline of key moments in boy band history:

1964: The Beatles appear on *The Ed Sullivan Show* in February 1964.

1966: The Monkees' (left) series first appears on TV, with the titular group eventually becoming a full-fledged band.

1968: The Jackson 5 sign to Motown Records, thus beginning the career of Michael Jackson.

1971: Years after appearing on TV singing barbershop music, another family boy band, the Osmonds, finally hit the top of the music charts with "One Bad Apple."

1977: In Puerto Rico, another hugely popular boy band forms: Menudo; none other than Ricky Martin would join the lineup in the '80s.

1983: New Edition's debut, *Candy Girl*, is released; the title track even bests Michael Jackson on the *Billboard* charts for a time.

1988: Four years after they first form, New Kids On The Block find a hit with *Hangin' Tough*; a year later, it had sold 7 million copies.

1990: Across the pond, in the UK, Take That forms, featuring singer Robbie Williams; by 1995 they go to No. 1 in the UK (No. 7 in the US) with their single "Back for Good." They break up a few years later.

1991: Boyz II Men's debut album is released; a year later, their song "End of the Road" ties an Elvis Presley record for longest time spent by a single in the No. 1 spot.

1993: The Backstreet Boys begin their journey, modeling the success of NKOTB; by 1999, they had broken the record for biggest sales of a single in one week.

1997: The band of brothers known as Hanson dominate the charts with "Mmmbop."

1998: NSYNC comes on the scene, considered competitors with Backstreet Boys (even though they have the same manager, Lou Pearlman); 98 Degrees, starring Nick Lachey and his brother Drew, is not far behind.

2000: Reality show *Making The Band* lands on MTV and begets O-Town, also managed by Lou Pearlman, who would be convicted of running a Ponzi scheme seven years later.

2005: The Jonas Brothers, carrying on the familial patterns of the Osmonds and the Jackson 5, first come into the cultural consciousness; they break the years-long silence of boy bands, as many earlier groups had since gone on hiatus or broken up.

2010: Burgeoning UK monolith One Direction first debuts on *The X Factor*; individual members like Zayn Malik and Harry Styles have since gone on to successful solo careers.

2018: BTS largely introduces a new style of boy band music, K-pop, to the States as their album *Love Yourself: Tear* hits No. 1, beginning the domination of the genre that currently has a stronghold on the industry.

RIGHT: The New Kids with Maurice Starr, circa 1990.

OPPOSITE PAGE: The New Kids, circa 1989.

these years later. In 2019, as Maurice battled health issues, all five New Kids were by their former producer/manager's bedside, with Donnie even posting about the occasion on his official social media channels. "It would be very hard to fully explain the impact this man has had on my life—on so many of our lives—beyond the success that he helped me to find professionally," he shared. "I can only say that if every kid on earth had someone to believe in them, the way that this man genuinely believed in (and fought for) me, the world would have nothing but love."

Returning to New York's famed Apollo Theatre in 2018 (a venue Maurice booked them to play early on in their career) for a show to celebrate the thirtieth anniversary of *Hangin' Tough,* Jordan Knight also took a moment to share his thoughts on Maurice, tapping into his characteristic "sensitive" side with an emotional speech. "Not only did Maurice get us on this stage, get us in the studio, believe in us, get us off the street . . . we would literally not be here tonight without that man," Jordan said, fighting back tears. "What I'm saying is, not only did he get us on these stages and get us in front of executives and get us our record deal and get us on Tiffany's tour . . . he also wrote the most beautiful damn music ever."

Though, if you asked Maurice, it was the New Kids themselves who deserve the credit. In a throwback photo posted to his Instagram page in 2018, he referred to them as "the five hardest working kids in show business" and said, "New Kids On The Block worked hard and deserve all the success they achieved and MORE!"

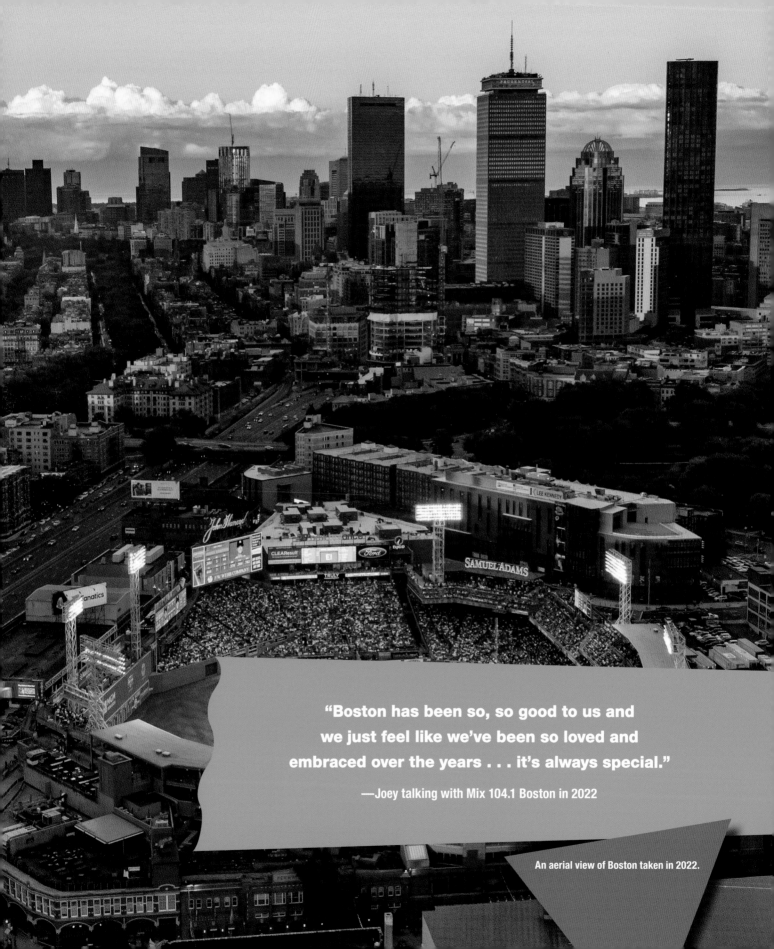

"Boston has been so, so good to us and
we just feel like we've been so loved and
embraced over the years . . . it's always special."

—Joey talking with Mix 104.1 Boston in 2022

An aerial view of Boston taken in 2022.

CHAPTER TWO

BORN IN BOSTON

New Kids On The Block bleed with Boston pride. From their uniquely Bostonian accents to their undying love of the Celtics and the Red Sox, all five of the members continue to be hometown heroes in good and bad times.

That includes career high moments such as playing the historic Red Sox baseball stadium Fenway Park three times, in 2011, 2017, and 2021. But it also includes participating in the Boston Strong charity concert, alongside other Beantown acts like Aerosmith and Dropkick Murphys, in 2013, shortly after the bombing at the Boston Marathon that devastated residents of the city, if not the entire country.

The horrific event was personally chilling for Joey, who had participated in the marathon that year and had finished the race just ten minutes prior to the bombs going off. "I happened to be on a bench in Copley Plaza, Copley Square," Joey said during the Boston Strong show, "but I don't care where you were that day, because this happened to all of us."

Most of the members of NKOTB grew up in the outlying area of the city known as Dorchester. It's the same part of town where the infamous Strand Nightclub is located, the spot where Maurice Starr once hosted his Hollywood Talent Nights in his searches for the next big act to come from the Massachusetts music mecca.

Dorchester is considered the largest neighborhood in Boston, covering six square miles, and it's also the oldest, having been established in 1630 by Puritans who had come from Dorchester, England, according to Boston University. They named the region after their beloved homeland. It is the epicenter of countless moments in American history, as the region where "America's first town meeting was

The Boston skyline at sunset in the late 1990s, featuring Prudential Tower (center).

held," and the site of the country's original free public school, Mather Elementary.

Dorchester is also known for being an incredibly diverse town—there was a large population of European immigrants, as seen in the makeup of the members of New Kids On The Block: Joey is Irish; Jordan and Jonathan are Canadian; Danny is Irish and Portuguese; and Donnie is a mix of Irish, Swedish, French, and English. But between the 1950s and 1980s, UMass notes there was a large shift in population, as more Black Americans were coming to Dorchester from the south, as well as natives of Asian and Caribbean countries.

The Boston that NKOTB grew up in during the 1970s and '80s was a gritty metropolis, one that was coming out of a post-war haze when many families had eyed the suburbs and uprooted. In fact, the National Bureau of Economic Research says that, by the 1980s, middle-class, blue-collar Boston was sharply on the decline, having lost nearly a third of its population, and real estate evaluations "were so low that three quarters of its homes were worth less than the bricks and mortar cost of construction," says NBER.

"When I was growing up, [Dorchester] was lower-middle-class. Now, of course, you can't get in there. The streets of my neighborhood are like a storybook. But when I was a kid, every house needed a paint job," Joey told *Boston Magazine* in an interview in 2021, talking about the Jamaica Plain part of Dorchester that he grew up in.

It was this hard-knocks landscape that laid out a bedrock for a burgeoning music scene. In fact, in the 1970s and '80s, Boston was known as a punk and rock haven, where bands like the Pixies and the Cars dominated the club circuit, drawing in Beantown's disaffected youth and a sense of rebellion—it's a legacy that would continue with working-class bards like the Dropkick Murphys, who were founded in Boston in the 1990s, known as much for their political views and pro-union sentiments as they are their decidedly Irish-style sound.

But there was also a groundswell of R&B coming out of Boston in the early '80s. It was largely indebted to the influence of Maurice Starr and his brothers in the Jonzun Crew who, after trying their hand at their own music, "saw themselves as old-fashioned star makers," says *Boston.com*—and soon enough, Maurice realized that vision with the New Kids. Adds the article, "The boy-band era was upon us, and you can credit (or blame) Boston for that one."

The R&B influence of New Kids On The Block arguably comes from the unique environment Donnie, Danny, Jordan, and Jonathan experienced in elementary school. In the '70s and '80s, Boston was piloting a highly controversial program to desegregate the city's schools, and the four boys were bussed to nearby Roxbury, a predominantly Black neighborhood located about a half-hour bus ride away. Those rides were seminal to establishing the friendship that would carry over to New Kids On The Block. The four budding talents attended William Monroe Trotter School, and according to *Biography.com*, it's here that all of them, Donnie in particular, became immersed in the rap and soul music their friends and classmates were listening to, often sharing headphones on the extended bus rides to and from school.

As Donnie told *Variety* in 2019, "We were . . . exposed to music and culture that we might not have been otherwise. We never felt out of our environment and we certainly wouldn't be here if not for those times. They intended to bring people together to learn about each other and be exposed to different things and that's what happened to us."

Danny Wood also expounded on his informative schooling environment in an interview with the *Boston Globe* in 2012,

sharing, "Outside of school, it was a very controversial time, because busing started when Donnie and I went into first grade. We were surrounded by chaos but in school it was amazing. We didn't feel all that. Everyone was open to being around everyone else."

Not only did the busing program influence NKOTB's eventual style—with the band members telling *Rolling Stone* some of their biggest musical heroes were Public Enemy, James Brown, Michael Jackson, and even Maurice Starr's former protégés New Edition—but in later years, the growing familiarity with Roxbury (where Maurice lived) helped the young teenagers become comfortable with routinely traveling to the town to work with their future producer.

The New Kids spent their youth—and pivotal time rehearsing—at the Dorchester Youth Collaborative, a safe place for teenagers

A banner at Fenway Park when New Kids On The Block performed there in July 2017.

BOSTON'S FINEST

While Chicago may be home of the blues, Detroit the birthplace of Motown, and Seattle the epicenter of grunge, Boston's music history is more of a mixed bag of R&B, soul, punk rock, and everything in between. Here are some of the greatest to hail from Beantown:

Godsmack: Toeing the line between grunge rock and nu metal, the heavy metal quartet has dominated radio with songs like "Speak" and often toured with Ozzfest.

The Lemonheads: A huge beacon of the indie rock style, the group led by Evan Dando became a hallmark of the '90s with albums like *It's a Shame About Ray*.

The Mighty Mighty Bosstones: These ska legends flipped the switch on punk rock with a full horn section that decorated songs like "The Impression That I Get."

New Edition: The predecessor to New Kids On The Block, Bobby Brown and co. were considered one of the original boy bands with hits like "Candy Girl."

The Pixies (below): One of the most enduring and celebrated rock bands of all time, the alt rock gods got their start at the University of Massachusetts and eventually even inspired Nirvana's Kurt Cobain with their "loud/quiet/loud" style.

Aerosmith (above): One of the biggest stadium bands of the 1970s that morphed from glam rock to include notes of heavy metal and blues with songs like "Dream On."

Boston: As their name might suggest, the classic prog rockers were born in their namesake city in the early 1970s.

The Cars: As new wave took over in the late '70s and '80s, the "Just What I Needed" hitmakers were a big part of the scene.

Dropkick Murphys: The Celtic punk rockers tap into Boston's strong Irish heritage with raucous jigs made for the working class.

Extreme: When the glam rockers released "More Than Words" in 1990, it set the standard for rock ballads of the future. Guitarist Nuno Bettencourt has also been a go-to session musician for acts like Rihanna.

to gather and be immersed in extracurricular activities, to deter them from entering gangs and taking part in other neighborhood violence around Boston. "We could've been out there on the streets doing nothing with our lives but we came up here and had a family," Donnie said to a group gathered at DYC in a TeenVid from the early '90s. "Up here you're sheltered not only by the building but by the positive state of mind everyone has here." After reaching their heights of fame, the New Kids continued to give back to the DYC, meeting with some of the enrollees and once making a $15,000 donation in the early '90s to keep the center going for future generations.

Over the years, no matter where their career took them, the New Kids have always very much been children of Boston, so much so that former Massachusetts governor Michael Dukakis declared an official New Kids On The Block Day on April 24, 1989—it's a holiday that's still celebrated on this date every year by the band and fans. In 2023, that celebration included marking the occasion with the release of new live versions of "You Got It (The Right Stuff)," "Please Don't Go Girl," "Cover Girl," "I'll Be Lovin' You (Forever)," and "Block Party" on streaming platforms.

Notably, in 2021, NKOTB further put their heritage on display, teaming up with fellow Bostonians New Edition for a "Battle of Boston" showdown at the televised American Music Awards, where each act traded turns performing their biggest hits in a ten-minute segment. It not only showed the East Coast town's musical legacy in full view but also hinted at its long-reaching tentacles—in the audience, K-pop boy band BTS were seen dancing along. By the end of the performance, the entire crowd was on its feet to offer a standing ovation.

Members of NKOTB and Boyz II Men onstage at the Boston Strong Concert in 2013, showing Boston pride.

"It's the combined thing that makes us work so good, everyone's different. . . . If one person leaves the group, I don't think it would ever be the same."

—Jordan talking to Boston TV station WBZ TV4 in 1989

The New Kids pose for a group portrait in New York in the late 1980s.

CHAPTER THREE

HELLO MY NAME IS . . .

In every boy band, the group's chemistry—and fan appeal—is often reliant on the different, distinctive characters behind each member. It can seem almost formulaic, as many of these pop groups often have the same starting lineup, typically offering the bad boy, the shy type, and the baby of the group, among other archetypes. Fans clamor for their personal favorites, usually discernable in the scream-o-meter levels at concerts as cameras pan over each individual member. You could say that New Kids On The Block set the mold for other groups to follow, presenting five very different guys who always made perfect sense together.

DONNIE
THE BAD BOY

Donnie was the first to join New Kids On The Block in 1984 when he was fifteen years old. Born August 17, 1969, Donnie was the eighth child of Alma and Donald Wahlberg. A ninth sibling, his baby brother, Mark, would complete the family two years later.

The large Irish-Catholic family (with other bits of European heritage thrown in) was of modest means. Both parents worked—Donald Sr. was a Teamsters truck driver, while Alma was employed by St. Margaret Hospital as a nurse's assistant—but even then it was often hard to provide for all the Wahlberg children. According to *Biography.com*, Alma once said,

Donnie, circa 1989.

"When I think about it now, I realize how hard it was, but back then we never even realized it! We thought everyone had all these kids, everyone lived like this." Certainly, all the New Kids lived that way, at least, with each member hailing from a family of six or more children, and all of them also very religious.

In a 2015 interview with *CBS This Morning*, Donnie shared more about the circumstances the family weathered and how it made him grateful for the success he found over the years. "My father drove a truck, was laid off half the time, or on strike the other half. Everything I get to do, I'm a kid in a candy store, I'm very blessed." He also told *Today.com* that there was always the chance of "having the lights or water turned off at any moment" and in other interviews he spoke of being on food stamps and learning the lessons of a brother who was incarcerated in the '80s for drug offenses.

Though the family unit was initially solid, always going to church together on Sundays, it also soon found its cracks. Donald Sr. and Alma divorced in 1982, just a few years before Donnie joined the New Kids. The two youngest boys, Donnie and Mark, went to live with Alma, while some of the other siblings moved in with Donald Sr. and a few others, already adults, lived on their own. (Many of the siblings and mom Alma would appear on the popular A&E reality show, *Wahlburgers*, years later, profiling the rise of their family burger chain.)

Around the time of his parents' divorce, Donnie started getting in some youthful trouble, racking up a rap sheet full of petty shoplifting, which first started to ink his bad boy image. But he also turned to music in tough times, and the new influences he was finding through friends in school, including rap, soul, and R&B, soon put a bug in his ear. It's said that Michael Jackson was one of his biggest influences, with Donnie quickly learning how to moonwalk and buying his own red leather jacket.

By the age of ten, Donnie was already trying to make a go of it as an official band member, in the short-lived group Risk; soon, he and good friend Danny Wood were breakdancing and writing their own rap lyrics, too. And when they advanced to Copley High School, they co-founded the hip-hop group the Kool Aid Bunch, shortly before the opportunity with Maurice Starr came knocking.

During his NKOTB audition, Donnie's ability to improv rhymes impressed Maurice so much that he was asked to join on the spot. "When I told him I needed some music, he started clapping his hands. I did one of my best spontaneous raps ever," Donnie told *People* in 1990. "I swore in it and in the next line, made up a line apologizing for swearing. Then here's

Maurice Starr, this famous guy, telling me . . . that I was one of the best rappers he ever heard. I mean, it was like, 'Are you serious?'"

The teenager was instrumental in shaping the band, since it was mostly his suggested friends who eventually completed the troupe. Over the years, Donnie continued to take on this leadership role in the group, if not also a "black sheep" persona, with his bad boy image a stark contrast to the other squeaky-clean teenagers.

Donnie rode a motorcycle, was often shirtless, had provocative dance moves, and was frequently cited for his role in brawls (including one on an airplane). "I don't understand why having an earring in your nose and sideburns and a beard and wearing a bandana makes you a bad one," he told *Entertainment Tonight* in 1990. "All these incidents you hear about, it's not nothing new. I mean, growing up, I had fights all the time. I had incidents all the time. But now I'm a New Kid

On The Block, I'm famous, and the press has given us this goody-two-shoes image that now, you know, everyone wants to say, 'Oh the New Kids aren't good after all.' But we never claimed to be good. We just claimed to be positive."

JONATHAN AND JORDAN THE HEARTTHROB BROTHERS

The Knight brothers also lived in Dorchester, where they were born, but their family had deep Canadian roots. Both of their parents, Allan and Marlene, hailed from Ontario and moved to the States when they were in their twenties and first starting their family. As such, Jonathan and Jordan both have dual citizenship and often spent summers in the Great White North.

"My grandfather had a cottage that he built by hand on Lake Erie and we used to stay there every summer with my aunts, uncles, and cousins. We'd play cards at night, walk along

The Knight brothers, circa 1989.

the beach looking for frogs and lizards, and surfboard," Jordan told *HuffPost Canada* back in 2012. He also told *North Stars* that same year that going to visit family up north was a reality check that put the Boston brothers in their place. "Every time we would come up to Canada—we were from the inner city of Boston and we had attitude and egos and everything else—our cousins would look at us and just laugh. 'You guys are so full of yourselves.'"

Jordan was born May 17, 1970, while his older brother Jonathan was born November 29, 1968, making the latter the eldest member of NKOTB by a hair. The boys had three other biological siblings; an adopted brother, Christopher; and a number of other foster siblings and live-in visitors that the Knight parents took in to provide them with shelter and resources. "There was mentally ill people and elderly people in my home my mom took care of," Jordan said in an appearance on *George Stroumboulopoulos Tonight*. In the

interview, Jordan also talks about their adopted brother, Chris, who is Black, which led Jordan and Jonathan to experience racism as young children. Jordan recalled a time they went to an ice-skating rink in South Boston and came out to find the family's car tires slashed.

The Knight brothers grew up in and around the church. Their father worked as a clergy member in an Episcopalian congregation (their mother, Marlene, was a social worker) and both Jordan and Jonathan sang in the choir. "I started singing really young, [at] five or six years old. I started in choirs and singing around the house. We would go to church, and I would hear the choir sing. I would sing all the songs after church. I begged my mother to get me in the church choir," Jordan told *Fusion Radio*, adding that he had a keyboard in his bedroom as a teen and loved the Beatles and the Stylistics, though he'd try to play all the hits on the radio by ear, too.

Jordan also sang in the school chorus while at William Monroe Trotter School, where he and Jonathan first met Donnie and Danny. Jordan's singing abilities stuck out to Donnie even years later—when Donnie was recommending additional members for the group that would

TOP: Jonathan, circa 1989.

BOTTOM: Jordan at the Kids' Choice Awards 1989.

become NKOTB, Jordan came to mind. "When Donnie met Maurice, I guess Donnie was thinking, 'Remember Jordan from school, he was always singing in the chorus," Jordan told *George Stroumboulopoulos Tonight.* "So he called me . . . and he was like, 'I'm in this group . . . this isn't like school chorus or church choir, this is the real deal.' So I went to try out . . . Maurice heard me sing a couple of notes, I don't even know how impressed he was but he was like, 'Yeah, alright, you're in.'" Jordan was just fourteen years old at the time.

Jonathan told *Live with Regis and Kathie Lee* in 1991 that he found out about the burgeoning NKOTB project from Jordan. "He came home and was bragging all about it, and I said, 'Well you're not leaving me out of this.'" Marlene, in fact, called Maurice and told him that her other son wanted to be in the group too, and soon, Jonathan got his own audition. He was sixteen years old at the time. "I actually didn't think I was going to make it because I just thought it's too good to be true," Jonathan added.

Though they had the same DNA, the two Knights started coming into very different personalities. Jordan was outgoing and not afraid to show emotion, with his sweet falsetto voice and sensitive demeanor soon giving him the reputation of "everyone's boyfriend." On the other hand, Jonathan was quieter and shyer, and he remained the more mysterious one in the group. When he officially came out in 2011, the news that he was gay shocked the fan base, after years of Jonathan keeping his truth ultra-secret to avoid hurting the band and their fame.

Jonathan's quiet demeanor was also due to strong bouts with a panic disorder, which ultimately led to him being the first member to leave NKOTB in 1994, a move that eventually culminated in the band's official breakup. In an *Oprah Winfrey Show* interview in 2001, Jordan revealed he had anxiety as well, but not to as large a degree as his brother. As Jonathan told Oprah, "The whole New Kids thing was crazy. The more it grew, the more I felt like I was trapped."

DANNY THE ATHLETE

While Danny had a great voice, too, what impressed Maurice Starr was that Danny was a nimble breakdancer (he also eventually became a choreographer for NKOTB). Dancing came naturally to Danny, who had been an athlete most of his life. "I've always been into fitness, it's my lifestyle, for me it's habit," he shared in an "inside look" video posted to his YouTube page in 2016, which showed him starting boxing sessions. According to the *Seattle Times*, which published an excerpt of the book, *The Lives and Loves of New Kids on the Block*, in 1990; Danny participated in school sports,

Danny, circa 1989.

loving track in particular but also playing basketball and soccer. As a teen, he migrated more into dancing and hip-hop culture with his best friend Donnie.

As Donnie told the *Boston Globe* in 2012, he and Danny started writing their own material and hosting rap performances and shows for their friends. By their sophomore year of high school, Danny and Donnie would go to the Catholic school dances every Friday night to bust a move. "We would be the two hip-hop guys, and they'd be like, 'Where did these guys come from?' In those neighborhoods, the guys didn't dare do anything like that. That wasn't cool. But me and Danny came in and turned the place upside down. There'd be a big circle, and we'd be breakdancing in the middle of it, and all the girls loved us."

Danny was born May 14, 1969, the first boy in the Wood family after three older sisters (two more siblings came later). Like the other New Kids, Danny came from modest means and a big religious family, and when they went to church on Sundays, all the Wood kids sang in the choir. His parents, Daniel Sr. and Elizabeth, worked for the postal service and Boston Public Schools, respectively. His Portuguese mother, nicknamed Betty, was a huge beacon in Danny's life, and was very encouraging in the beginning. He shared a memory with *Entertainment Tonight* of writing the 1988 hit "I'll Be Loving You (Forever)," recalling bringing home the demo to his mom, who voiced her approval.

"My mom always knew I was in this group and that we were making music, but I don't think she took it seriously until she heard that song. Then she was like, 'You guys have got a hit!'" Danny shared. When the Wood family matriarch passed away from breast cancer in 1999, Danny was so impacted by her loss he created the Remember Betty foundation to raise funds to provide support to other families battling the illness.

Danny also loved school as a child. His first day of kindergarten was when he met Donnie, and they were inseparable from that day forward. When Donnie recommended Danny for the burgeoning New Kids On The Block group, Danny was hesitant at first. While the opportunity sounded exciting, the high-schooler had also just been offered a full-ride scholarship to attend Boston University to continue his studies (in fact, Danny is the only New Kid who had been accepted to college).

As the boy band started finding fame a couple years later, Danny tried to do both, taking college courses by day and working with the band at night. He'd spend hours in the studio, becoming more and more of an engineer/gear head, but it soon became apparent he was burning the candle at both ends and couldn't sustain the lifestyle. As the book *The Lives and Loves of New Kids on the Block* reveals, Danny remembered, "The dean just said, 'Look, your heart is with the group and it could be a once-in-a-lifetime opportunity. Go with it; your scholarship will always be waiting for you if you want to come back. You're not going to lose it.'"

JOEY THE BABY

Joey was the final addition to the group and, at first, he stuck out like a sore thumb. He was several years the junior of the other members (born December 31, 1972) and from another neighborhood, Jamaica Plain, meaning he had work to do to break through the ironclad bond of the other four schoolyard friends.

CHAPTER FOUR

TEEN SENSATIONS

To understand the incredible fandom that exploded around New Kids On The Block in the latter part of the 1980s and into the early '90s—a time in which they reportedly received around 30,000 fan letters a day— takes some context. Certain trends and lifestyles became paramount for kids and teens in Generation X (those born between 1965 and 1980). This precious era was before the internet, before social media, before memes and TikTok, before even cell phones became a normal part of daily life.

In the 1980s, youth trends were shifting away from what their parents' generation had to offer, exemplified by more freedom to really slow down and explore all the trials and tribulations of teenagehood, set to an incredible soundtrack made by their peers as well as therapeutic coming-of-age movies.

In the decades prior to the 1980s, young people "grew up" very quickly. They may have been drafted by the Armed Forces to fight in heavy conflicts of the time, like the Vietnam War (men as young as eighteen were called up), or perhaps they were acclimated to getting married and starting families early. In 1960, one in six women were under the age of eighteen when they wed, while 18 percent of men were under the age of twenty, according to data from the National Center for Family & Marriage Research. By 1990, those numbers fell to under 10 percent for each demographic. The 1980s also brought a large shift in the workforce, as many teens stopped going directly into trades post-high school and focused on enrolling in four-year college programs. Through much of the 1970s, the percentage of recent high school graduates enrolled in college wavered in the high 40 percentile; by 1991, that figure was 62.4 percent, according to records from the US Bureau of Labor Statistics.

As the *Saturday Evening Post* puts it, "Humans have been turning 13 for tens of thousands of years, but only recently did it occur to anybody that this was a special thing," adding that the idea of the teenager really emerged thanks to simultaneous trends in schooling, economics, and technological advancements. Namely, high school culture was a place where teens could form their identities outside the family unit, post-war

economic boosts provided more disposable money for the family (passed down many times in allowances), and an eventual rise in car ownership for younger people became a way for them to have even more independence.

Entertainment was also starkly different. Color TVs weren't even in the majority of homes until the 1980s, nor was cable TV widely accepted until that time. Most bands in the 1950s and '60s found their footing with appearances on *The Ed Sullivan Show* and *American Bandstand*.

Everything changed literally overnight, when a new station called MTV debuted on August 1, 1981, and set off a cultural mushroom cloud. With programming relying on VJs (rather than DJs) and premiering music videos rather than

The Beatles on *The Ed Sullivan Show*.

Movies like *The Breakfast Club* spoke to '80s teens.

just audio tracks, MTV took the long tradition of radio and gave it a dimensional, visual makeover that had mass appeal—and had teens glued to their TVs. Enter the "MTV generation."

"By the mid-1980s, MTV had produced a noticeable effect on motion pictures, commercials, and television," notes *Britannica.com*. "It also changed the music industry; looking good (or at least interesting) on MTV became as important as sounding good when it came to selling recordings."

Syracuse University professor Robert Thompson told ABC's *Good Morning America* how this translated even more to young people: "MTV, essentially, in 1981 was waiting with open arms for all those kids who had learned to count and who had learned their alphabet on the spectacular hallucinogenic imagery of *Sesame Street*. MTV was ready to embrace them into early adulthood."

In the case of New Kids On The Block, they may not have even found their future success

without the channel's influence. Though their first music video, made in 1988 for *Hangin' Tough's* lead single "Please Don't Go Girl," failed to track at the time, their second video for "You Got It (The Right Stuff)" went into heavy circulation on MTV months later, leading to the band's invitation to appear on *Club MTV*, a modern version of *American Bandstand* in which the music group performed their hit song to a crowd of dancing teens.

By the early part of 1989, the exposure paid off, with "You Got It (The Right Stuff)" cracking *Billboard*'s Top 10, NKOTB's first song to do so. Five more tracks from the *Hangin' Tough* album would follow suit in 1989. And, over time, the group would continue to turn to music videos as part of their release strategy. They've created twenty-eight music videos as of 2023, the latest being for 2022's "Bring Back The Time."

Beyond MTV's effects for shaping massive music stars of the day, the other element New

Kids On The Block got wrapped into was the teen idol phenomenon that ran rampant in the 1980s as young people became huge consumers of entertainment.

In 1978, 74% of the moviegoing audience was between the ages of twelve and twenty-nine, says author James King in his book, *The Ultimate History of the '80s Teen Movie*, as reported on by *PopMatters*. The shifting demographic resulted largely in the teen movie genre, with films like *Ferris Bueller's Day Off* to *Say Anything* dominating movie screens.

It helped that, like leading actors of the day, all members of New Kids On The Block were in the same age group as their fans (ranging from twelve to sixteen years old when they first started). They were seen as contemporaries and "could-be" friends and boyfriends of those who worshipped them. As the *New York Times* reported in 1990, "Most of the group's fans say the same thing: 'The New Kids are ours, they're our age, they understand us and we understand them.'"

It was the same appeal as the Coreys (Corey Feldman and Corey Haim), who found fame with movies like *The Goonies*, or the Brat Pack (Rob Lowe, Molly Ringwald, Judd Nelson, Emilio Estevez, et al.) who appeared in countless coming-of-age movies during the decade. In music, the '80s-era teen idol crowns were worn by Debbie Gibson and Tiffany in addition to New Kids On The Block.

Not only were these teen stars the same age as the fans who loved them, but the movies and shows and songs they were part of told "everyday" stories. The whole body of work of John Hughes spoke to this—how much more normal of a story could there be besides getting detention or dealing

with family drama? In the case of New Kids, what's more relatable (and aspirational) than a bunch of working-class Boston kids with thick accents and wide smiles who somehow made it to the top of the charts?

It was a storyline that was told ad nauseum in a slew of teen-focused magazines that picked up great steam in the '80s, with New Kids On The Block becoming constant centerfolds and poster tear-outs in the likes of *Tiger Beat, Bop, Wow!, 16, Teen Beat,* and the like. These magazines could best be described as G-rated *Playboy* for teens, who'd scoop them up, rip out the pages, and fix them to their walls with Scotch tape, in order to wake up and go to bed beside their favorite idols every day and night.

In honor of *Tiger Beat*'s fiftieth anniversary in 2015, *Buzzfeed News* explored its cultural impact on teens, in relation to the salacious celebrity rag mags of the day that catered to adults. "'Tiger' was slang for 'cute boy'; 'beat' indicated how central music . . . would be to the magazine. And unlike the fan mags broadcasting Liz Taylor and Richard Burton's latest romp, *Tiger Beat* kept its content strictly PG—there was never a hint of scandal or smut, just dreams of holding hands. The magazine was unabashed in its embrace of the teen audience and their sensibility: Every headline, even the most banal, ended with a flourish of punctuation, such as, 'David ordered a steak!'"

Though it's hard to estimate how many times New Kids On The Block appeared within the pages of the teen magazines during their heyday, one eager seller on Etsy once posted her collection of clippings for sale, totaling nearly 250 pages.

ALL MUSIC VIDEOS, ALL THE TIME

Capitalizing on the success of one of their earliest music videos—for "You Got It (The Right Stuff)" in 1988—New Kids On The Block made it standard practice to create stylized videos for nearly all their singles over the past 40 years. In fact, their most recent, for the 2022 track, "Bring Back the Time," spoofs other music videos of the '80s era with visual references to Devo, A Flock Of Seagulls, Billy Idol, Robert Palmer, and Twisted Sister, among others. Here's a chronological list of all NKOTB videos released from 1988 to 2023:

1. "Please Don't Go Girl"
2. "You Got It (The Right Stuff)"
3. "I'll Be Loving You (Forever)"
4. "Hangin' Tough"
5. "Didn't I (Blow Your Mind) (Live)"
6. "Cover Girl"
7. "This One's For The Children" (below)
8. "Step By Step"
9. "Valentine Girl (Live)"
10. "Tonight"
11. "Games"
12. "Call It What You Want"
13. "Baby, I Believe In You (Live)"
14. "If You Go Away"
15. "Never Let You Go"
16. "No More Games (Live)"
17. "Summertime"
18. "Single"
19. "2 In The Morning"
20. "Remix (I Like The)"
21. "The Whisper"
22. "I Need A Melody"
23. "One More Night"
24. "Thankful"
25. "Boys In The Band (Boy Band Anthem)"
26. "80s Baby"
27. "House Party"
28. "Bring Back The Time"

The New Kids in 1989.

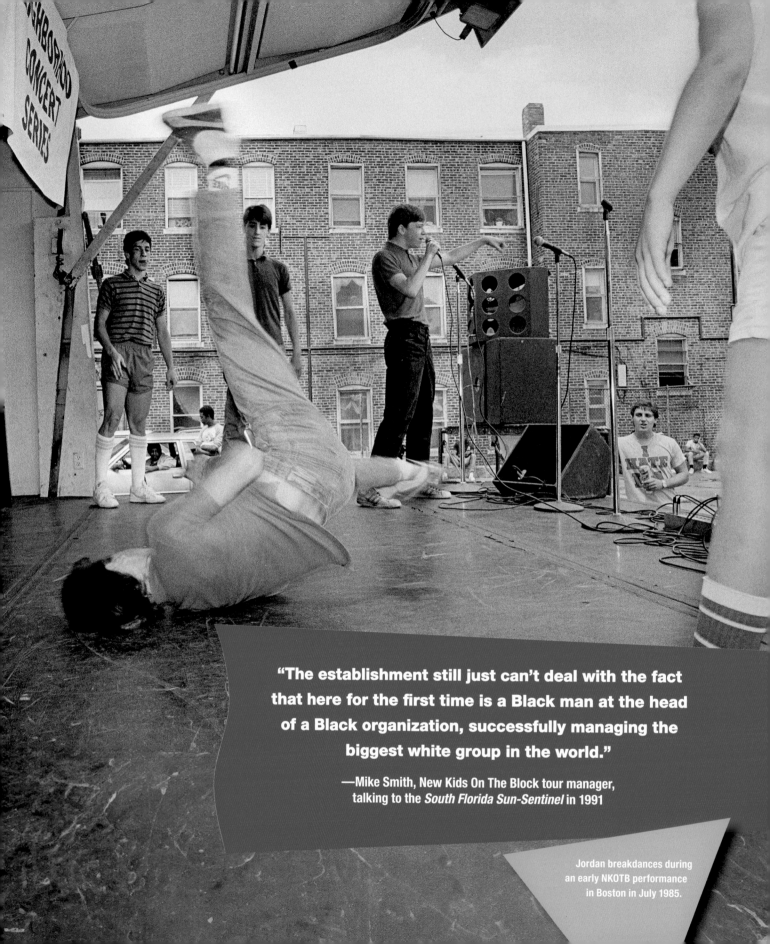

"The establishment still just can't deal with the fact that here for the first time is a Black man at the head of a Black organization, successfully managing the biggest white group in the world."

—Mike Smith, New Kids On The Block tour manager, talking to the *South Florida Sun-Sentinel* in 1991

Jordan breakdances during an early NKOTB performance in Boston in July 1985.

CHAPTER FIVE

A MATTER OF BLACK AND WHITE

New Kids On The Block certainly weren't the first band to cross the racial divide (nor did they do it particularly well in the beginning, as their debut album flop would soon show).

Sam Phillips, owner of the legendary label Sun Records, once famously said, "If I could find a white man who had the Negro sound and Negro feel, I could make a billion dollars"—and he did just that with Elvis Presley in 1950s.

A decade or so later, Led Zeppelin and the Rolling Stones would find inspiration from African-American blues artists and, unlike the original creators, were able to go mainstream with their music. Even in modern times, it's estimated that young, suburban white men and boys are 80 percent of the audience that listens to hip-hop. "This became a recognized industry fact in 1991, and since then, the music industry has crafted mainstream hip-hop culture to appeal to that demographic," says *Mic.com*.

So, when Maurice Starr went looking for five white teenagers who could expand on the success he had found with his former boy band, New Edition, it was just one step in a long appropriation trend that has become a part of the backbone of the music industry. However, Maurice's plan was to do the opposite of what had been done before—rather than draw white kids into traditionally Black music styles, he wanted to market New Kids On The Block to Black audiences. Maurice thought that by winning over Black music fans first, he could then attract white fans. He was largely inspired

Sun Records owner
Sam Phillips (left)
and Elvis Presley.

and James Brown—and he reported all five had recently read *The Autobiography of Malcolm X*.

"It's what I grew up on. I'm a hip-hop dude. If Maurice hadn't done this, I'd probably be making house records," Donnie told *New York Times* in 1990. "Because that's what I like, house and rap. Rap was what I listened to, from the Sugar Hill Gang's *Rapper's Delight* on; I was in the fourth grade. So, I'm just being me."

Maurice started to capitalize on his marketing plan—as a Black man and one who worked with young Black acts like New Edition, he believed he could help infuse his new act with the right cultural touchpoints, so he began to write all of New Kids' material himself and hired Black choreographers to help teach the teens more dance moves as they began rehearsals in the mid-1980s. In fact, their entire team and crew were all Black—not only Maurice but their other manager, Dick Scott, tour manager Peter Work, as well as their bodyguards and eventual live band. As *New York Times* stated, "For a white group to be produced and managed by Black [men] and for it to be hugely successful—is unprecedented."

NKOTB also rehearsed at a place called the Lee School, which was a community center for Black children, as Maurice told *New York Times*. "I put the band there to see the Black talent, to feel the vibe," he told the paper. "That's where the Kids learned dancing and singing," he added. "You can be Black and not be convincing, but to be white you have to be 1,000 times more convincing, so it was work. I made sure they made the right moves."

Regardless of the effort put in, Maurice had an incredibly difficult time getting New Kids On The Block any attention or a record deal in the beginning. "A white child act performing Black music seemed like a joke," the *New York Times*

by the "interracial marketing" of Motown Records, says *New York Times*.

Even though the members of NKOTB were starkly Irish and a variety of other European heritages, Maurice believed they had deep-rooted soul. "These [kids] are white kids who are Black," Starr told the *Los Angeles Times*. As discussed, Donnie, Danny, Jordan, and Jonathan went to school at William M. Trotter Elementary in the largely Black community of Roxbury, and it's here they became engrossed in rap, hip-hop, soul, R&B, street culture, and breakdancing.

In his profile for *Rolling Stone* in 1990, journalist David Wild commented how all the members "talk like veteran B-boys," noting they also waxed ecstatic about their favorite stars of the day—Michael Jackson, Public Enemy, opined, adding that Black radio programmers refused to play the music. Not only that, but because Nynuk (as the band was known at the time) was marketed as a teen group, radio in general was resistant to buy-in, believing that the right demo to listen to the music would be in school for much of the day that it would be played, which wouldn't appeal to its base of supportive advertisers.

After much persistence, Maurice caught the attention of Columbia Records executive Cecil Holmes who worked for the label's R&B division at the time. The first thing the label did was make the band change its moniker—New Kids On The Block was born from a rap Donnie wrote, and the name stuck. Columbia released the group's eponymous debut album in 1986 hoping for a hit, but it was a total flop. The bubblegum-pop song "Be My Girl" was the first single released, but beyond some local airplay on Boston radio, it failed to track nationwide.

"Stop It Girl" came next and gained even less attention. The whole album moved only a meager 20,000 copies. Maurice and NKOTB were at a crucial impasse.

Continuing to believe in their appeal, Maurice went overboard on booking the band anywhere he could to get some traction, starting regionally—and often to disastrous results. Some of their first gigs were in small clubs and schools around Boston, which catered to moms and their daughters (there were even popcorn and soda concessions). Then came malls, state fairs, and retirement homes. In the beginning, they couldn't afford a live band, so New Kids played to tracks, making the whole thing seem even more amateur.

One of their earliest gigs was performing for a few hundred incarcerated men at the Deer Island Prison near Boston Harbor, where one of Donnie's brothers was serving a sentence. Soon after came a gig at the Kite Festival in

LEFT: Donnie poses with manager Dick Scott, circa 1989.

RIGHT: Maurice Starr talks to a crowd at a Roxbury middle school after a performance by Starr's latest musical endeavor, HeartBeat Boys.

A LESS THAN PERFECT DEBUT

The first album from New Kids On The Block was meant to introduce them to the masses. Self-titled with the band's name, the cover art likewise brings viewers up close and personal with all five members as they play around a street sign in their native Boston. Each of the five guys is smiling and wearing trademark '80s clothing—oversized, striped, long-sleeved shirts, cartoon tees, and bright, geo metric-print sweaters.

New Kids On The Block was released on April 1, 1986, and though it wasn't meant to be an April Fool's joke, the album in so many ways became one, as it barely moved the needle with sales or radio pickup. It didn't even crack the *Billboard 200* charts upon its release and reportedly only sold 20,000 copies.

Almost all the album's ten songs were written by producer/manager Maurice Starr, with the exception of "New Kids On The Block"—that was a rap that Donnie wrote while the band was still called Nynuk. With pressure from their label, Columbia Records, to change the band name, soon the band's moniker was changed to match.

All five members shared vocal duties on tracks, including "Are You Down?" and "I Wanna Be Loved By You," while Donnie is the lead on his all-important rap track as well as "Be My Girl." Joey is prominent on "Treat Me Right" and Jordan took the reins on "Didn't I (Blow Your Mind)," a cover of a 1969 song from the R&B/soul group the Delfonics, who hailed from nearby Philadelphia. Back in the late '60s, the Delfonics had a hit with the track, as it broke the Top 10 of the *Billboard* charts.

The NKOTB album debut also includes "Stop It Girl," notable for featuring a rap verse from former member Mark Wahlberg. Elsewhere on the record, members are paired to share vocal leads on songs such as "Popsicle," "Angel," and "Don't Give Up On Me." As can be discerned from the song titles, many of them relied on outgrown bubblegum-pop tactics.

Though there are few early reviews of the album from 1986, guest comments on the site *Rate Your Music* lament the dated synthesizers, "atrocious lyrical work," "silly love songs," and "hilarious attempts at early hip-hop" that appear on the record.

But there was life to it yet. After New Kids On The Block found their footing with *Hangin' Tough* in 1989, Columbia Records decided to give the debut album another try. They re-released "Didn't I (Blow Your Mind)" as a single and fans quickly caught onto it. The push eventually made *New Kids On The Block* go triple platinum in 1990, as certified by the Recording Industry Association of America® (RIAA), meaning it sold 3 million copies.

Franklin Park, which looked like the scene of a prison yard shakedown. It was NKOTB's biggest crowd yet, with estimations of 10,000 people. Hosted by a local radio station who handed out records to crowd members, the freebies were soon used as quasi weapons, hurled at the New Kids On The Block. Danny was even cut on the cheek by a flying disc. As bodyguards tried to pull the band members off stage to safety, Donnie insisted they go on (he saw a schoolmate in the crowd and didn't want to be embarrassed). This was the unsuccessful gig pattern for the first few years, but the band and Maurice remained committed.

A couple years later, in 1988, after their first music video for "Please Don't Go Girl" was pitched to the BET network, the band was booked for an appearance on *Showtime at the Apollo*'s famous "Amateur Night," held at the famed theater in New York's Harlem neighborhood. NKOTB members have described it as one of the "scariest" shows ever, with the anticipation of how the notoriously ruthless crowd might react to a bunch of white kids. Instead, the band received waves of applause, hollering cheers, and standing ovations by the end of "Please Don't Go Girl" and "You Got It (The Right Stuff)." Some in the crowd were even chanting, "Go, white boys!" It marked a huge turning point that started to show the band's burgeoning crossover appeal.

A portrait of New Kids On The Block posing backstage at Maurice Starr's Hollywood Talent Night event in Boston in January 1986.

New Kids On The Block perform during
a circa 1989 commercial shoot.

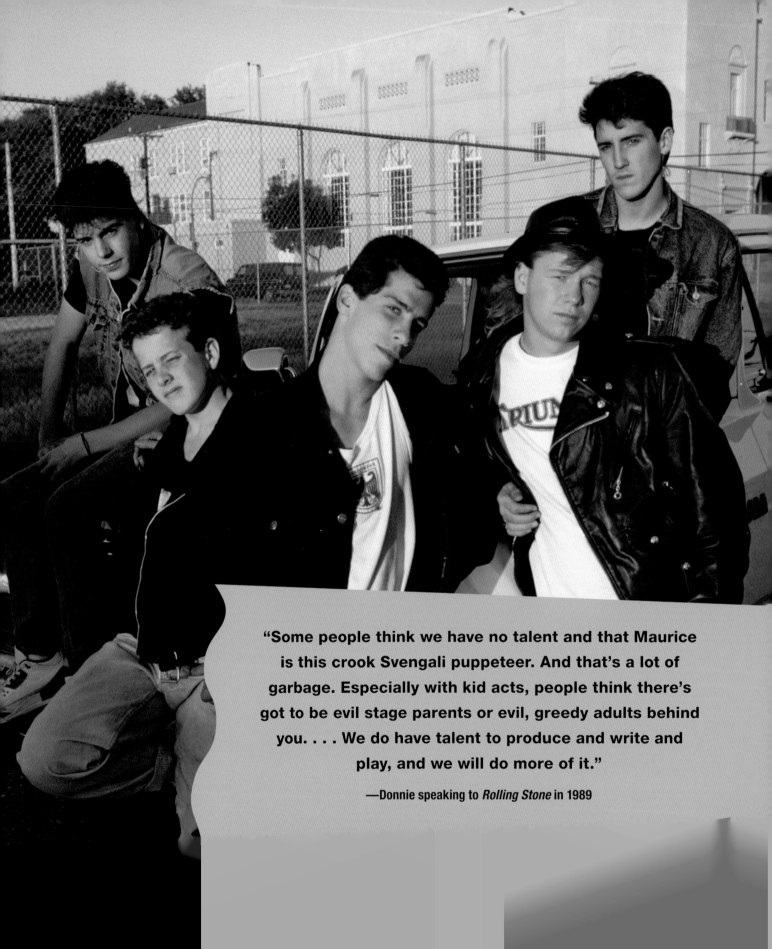

"Some people think we have no talent and that Maurice is this crook Svengali puppeteer. And that's a lot of garbage. Especially with kid acts, people think there's got to be evil stage parents or evil, greedy adults behind you. . . . We do have talent to produce and write and play, and we will do more of it."

—Donnie speaking to *Rolling Stone* in 1989

CHAPTER SIX

WHO ARE THE REAL NEW KIDS?

Things hit a boiling point after the band's debut album failed to track when it was released in 1986. Says *Billboard*, "Few people took notice, and those who did didn't seem to think the adolescent quintet would last for another album—much less another 30-plus-years."

In fact, Columbia Records considered dropping the group altogether and questioned Maurice Starr's marketing tactic to try to win over Black audiences with R&B/pop made by white teenagers. But the label's A&R rep and executive producer Cecil Holmes, who first gave NKOTB a recording contract, believed in the potential of the band and pushed for them to remain on the roster.

With a re-commitment from the label, the band went back into the "studio" (a makeshift recording room in the second story of Maurice's house in Roxbury, dubbed the House of Hits), for a good chunk of 1987 and part of 1988, working on their sophomore album which would eventually become *Hangin' Tough*.

Conditions were less than ideal for making a hit. Jordan described it in retrospect as a "dilapidated house" when he chatted with *Variety* in 2019, but also said, "To us, it was awesome. It was a playground." The room where they would work every day after school was full of holes in the walls and loose wires and no soundproofing, so they had to pause every time an ambulance or police car drove past, according to the article. When they did have down time between recording sessions, they'd take broken bats to play oversized ping-pong games on a court made of traffic barricades.

The New Kids perform in Boston in July 1985.

The New Kids, all of whom besides the youngest, Joey, were nearing the end of high school at the time, remained committed to the project—even as they worked jobs in the summer of 1987 in downtown Boston (Donnie and Danny worked at a bank, Jordan at a mailroom across the street). "From the summer of '87 on, we were together all the time. We were with Maurice or we'd go ride around and play basketball together. . . . Everything we did all day was related to the group," Donnie shared with biographer Nikki Van Noy, in a snippet from her book published in the *Boston Globe*. Alma Wahlberg also remembers that "the regimen was really tough," as she told *People*, with rehearsals every night after school and shows nearly every weekend.

But with their growing maturity as well as exposure to new kinds of music and '80s street culture, the New Kids started to question Maurice's instincts and clamored for more control over the project, including the direction of the new tunes. Donnie told *Rolling Stone* in 1989 that the New Kids were over "seeing themselves depicted in the mainstream press as talentless white kids being manipulated by a frustrated Black mastermind" and they took on a more active role beyond just assuming the singing and dancing parts they were assigned to.

Maurice was still involved, of course. He was the one who helped teach Danny Wood how to work mixing boards and engineer the album, and Maurice still wrote much of the material on *Hangin' Tough.* Except the New Kids didn't approve every song he brought to them. "The dynamic changed with *Hangin' Tough*," Donnie told *Rolling Stone* in 2018. "We took on more of a role. It stopped being Maurice trying to fit us into songs that sounded like the Osmonds, the Jacksons, or New Edition, and more about us identifying songs that fit us. He listened to us and he trusted us."

The result was that Donnie, Danny, and Jordan were all credited as associate producers on *Hangin' Tough*, with Danny also credited for programming, recording, mixing, and engineer work. It was a turning point for New Kids On The Block, and a move that forever changed the course of the band. By

trusting their instincts, they migrated away from Maurice's Motown instincts and created something fresh, something that they heard on their headphones and in the streets. They were teenagers, after all, so they were prime consumers of the most contemporary styles of music at the time and, by osmosis, it leaked into their new material and made them instantly relevant.

"We were involved more creatively with Maurice," Donnie told *PopStruck* in 2019, recalling the making of the second album. "We were influenced by R&B and hip-hop, hip-hop specifically more so than Maurice Starr, and I think our music on that album was really an amalgamation of hip-hop, pop, and R&B."

One of the songs that always sticks out to the New Kids from that album is the title track; though the members have often said it was the band's attempt to create a theme song for their

New Kids On The Block have been making our hearts beat fast since the 1980s.

THEY'VE GOT THE LOOK

Along with taking more ownership over the music of New Kids On The Block, the five teens also started dictating more of what their image was going to be. Gone were the open-mouthed smiles, cartoon T-shirts, and full-color photo that appeared on the album art for their self-titled debut. For *Hangin' Tough*'s cover art, the band appeared in a more edgy black-and-white photo on a subway train headed to Coney Island, wearing leather jackets, fedoras, hoodies, and beguiling smirks on their faces. If the name of the album alone didn't try to epitomize their "toughness" (in retaliation for being dubbed a boy band), the new look (below) sure went the distance.

The makeover appeared in the subsequent music videos for *Hangin' Tough* singles as well. In the accompanying piece for the title track, Donnie appears in a motorcycle jacket and ripped jeans and wears earrings with the beginnings of a rat tail; Danny has a fade haircut with sidelines; they're breakdancing, throwing around baseball bats, playing air guitar, and disrobing while the camera pans over to girls screaming. Donnie even throws around some suggestive hip thrusts and, by the end, unveils a T-shirt that reads "Home Boy."

In the video for "You Got It (The Right Stuff)," Donnie jumps into a moving convertible carrying the other four guys as they go on a joy ride. At one point, they drive over an industrial bridge while perched on top of the car. At another point, they're flirting with girls walking on the side of the road as the car whizzes by, only to do a U-turn to pick them up. They play hide-and-seek in a cemetery and Jordan dons a T-shirt of goth band Bauhaus. This clearly was not the same boy band that emerged two years prior.

The band would continue to play with their image over time, but the biggest transition happened in this period between *New Kids On The Block* and *Hangin' Tough* when, like their music, their entire style went through an overhaul and gave them more street cred—and screaming fans.

beloved Boston Celtics, there's also a part of "Hangin' Tough" that speaks to the band's own perseverance in challenging times. Maurice, who wrote the lyrics, has gone on record to say the song was about the rough times the band and team went through when the debut album tanked. In the interview with *PopStruck*, Donnie ultimately echoed that sentiment. "Hangin' Tough," he said, was "about the hustle and the grind that we were in back then. It takes me back to our roots."

The band's own influence on the project would soon be noticed. While their self-titled album was super clean-cut (they even rallied against cuss words in one track), with the material on *Hangin' Tough*, they "matured lyrically and certainly vocally," says *Billboard*. Plus, as the article pointed out, it helped that the band's image was starting to become more grown-up too. "They weren't exactly bad boys, but they had more of an edge than their squeaky-clean debut suggested."

INSET: *Hangin' Tough* on vinyl.

TOP: New Kids in a posed shot in 1988.

"All we wanted to do was prove we could go the distance—that we could make a record, stand up in the face of adversity, and earn some respect. We didn't necessarily think we would sell so many records or become a phenomenon. We just wanted to prove people wrong and show we belonged. Of course, when we finally arrived, we didn't prove it to everyone else . . . we proved it to ourselves."

—Donnie speaking to *Variety* in 2019

The New Kids photographed for *Teen Beat* in 1988.

CHAPTER SEVEN

THE STRENGTH OF HANGIN' TOUGH

While most bands can suffer what is referred to as the "sophomore slump"—bowing to the pressure when making a follow-up to a defining, career-making debut album—it was quite the opposite for New Kids On The Block. Perhaps they just needed to grease the wheels a bit, or perhaps what was needed were the instincts of the Kids themselves to help shape their sound and image. Either way, the group's second attempt at a hit record was a far superior effort than their very lukewarm debut. To call *Hangin' Tough* anything less than life-changing for both the band and for all of pop music would be a gross underestimation of its importance and longstanding appeal.

Over time, the 1988 album would go on to sell 14 million copies (7 million of them by the end of 1989 alone) and become certified 8x platinum by the Recording Industry Association of America® by the time the band released a thirtieth anniversary edition in 2019. According to *Rolling Stone*, sales of the album by late 1989 brought in roughly $30 million, a salve for its label in "what many predicted would be a dire fiscal year." *Hangin' Tough* remains New Kids' best-selling album, contributing largely to the band's 80 million records sold over the course of their five-decade career.

Though it might've gone nowhere without the attention of one radio DJ in Florida who singlehandedly helped propel New Kids On The Block into the mainstream.

Initially, Maurice Starr was still intent on trying to grow a fanbase of Black music consumers ahead of *Hangin' Tough*'s release by Columbia Records in August 1988—and the tactic continued to be problematic. The first pre-launch single that was settled upon was the R&B ballad "Please Don't Go Girl," heavily focusing on the Michael Jackson-esque falsetto of then-sixteen-year-old Joey McIntyre. The band's first music video was created for the song, financed with $9,000 of Maurice's own money and helmed by their early go-to visionary Doug Nichol. Doug told *Variety* of the video's importance, "It gave people [the first] visual of the group. We really captured their camaraderie and girls from all over the country fell in love with them from it."

The final product was sent to BET as well as traditionally Black radio stations across America in April 1988. It did nothing and the single barely moved. Again, New Kids On The Block seemed doomed to fail.

That is, until "Please Don't Go Girl" landed in the hands of Randy Kabrich, the program director at WRBQ-FM (Q-105) in Tampa, Florida. As the *Tampa Bay Times* recalls in a 1990 article, "Many insiders credit [Randy] for breaking the group on radio." Knowing the song was a hit, on a whim he added the track to the station's regular rotation (the first station to do so) and called his radio rep at

Columbia Records to encourage the label to promote the track, insisting it had mainstream appeal. Turns out his hunch was right.

Soon enough, listeners in Tampa Bay started calling into the station wanting to hear "Please Don't Go Girl"—one of them may have been Tampa-born Aaron Carter (he covered the song in 1997). In no short order, it became the station's most requested song. Other radio stations in the region and then nationally started to catch on and added "Please Don't Go Girl" to their rotations, as well, and the domino effect was in motion. Though Maurice's crossover plan failed, as the *Tampa Bay Times* says, with the new radio traction, "the New Kids were fed straight to the young white audience. Success didn't take long."

Columbia Records noticed and decided to put more promotion into the track and the band. The song hit No. 10 on the *Billboard Hot 100* singles chart, the band's first track to break the Top 10 and, nearly overnight, the New Kids entered their megastar incubation period. Four more singles (and subsequent music videos) from *Hangin' Tough* were released, each tracking even higher on the *Billboard* charts, including "You Got It (The Right Stuff)," released in November 1988, which went to No. 3; "I'll Be Loving You (Forever)," released in April 1989, and the title track, "Hangin' Tough," released in July 1989, both of which spent a week in the No. 1 spot; and "Cover Girl," which came out in August 1989 and safely landed at No. 2. MTV also started taking notice and put the music videos into regular play on the channel. The result: NKOTB was the first teen act that enjoyed five Top 10 hits from one album.

With the exception of the track "My Favorite Girl," which features writing credits for Donnie, Danny, and Jordan, all the songs on *Hangin'*

Tough were once again written by Maurice. He also played all the instruments himself and added some backup vocals. Curiously enough, as Jordan told *Variety*, the band's first No. 1 hit, "I'll Be Loving You (Forever)," was a track straight from Maurice's vaults that he'd written years before he started working with the New Kids—it was initially intended for Smokey Robinson.

"He had it kicking around and thought it would fit my voice well. As soon as he started playing it for me, it was just hauntingly beautiful," Jordan said, also describing the recording process of that track as something very similar to what Motown artists (Maurice's favorites) would often default to; namely, recording two vocal takes and layering both together to produce a "warmer sound."

Two other tracks—the album ender "Hold On" (featuring Danny on lead vocals for the first time) and Donnie-led rock-pop track "Cover Girl"—were slated for rock bands Maurice

started working with. But Donnie, again trying to help steer the group, recalled "begging" for the two tracks to be authorized for *Hangin' Tough*. "At that point, it was about finding the best material, not pigeonholing ourselves into songs about puppy love," he told *Variety*.

As the band started diversifying their material on *Hangin' Tough* (the title track even had a metal-tinged guitar solo), they also started discovering what kind of songs fit each guy's vocal range and personal style. In particular, Donnie was given "rougher" cuts that had some attitude to them; Jordan was prioritized for soulful ballads; Joey was the go-to for the high notes; and Danny and Jonathan helped fill in the gaps.

Over the course of 1988 and into 1989, *Hangin' Tough* continued its ascent. By the end of '89, and 7 million copies later, the album was one of the top sellers that year (the very top was *Don't Be Cruel*, the second solo album of former New Edition member and Maurice Starr

protégé Bobby Brown). During the album's run, the band was booked for appearances on *Soul Train*, Nickelodeon, and that famed night at the Apollo Theatre.

The sudden interest in NKOTB also compelled Columbia Records to try again with the group's maligned 1986 self-titled debut. Columbia put the New Kids song "Didn't I (Blow Your Mind)" back into the mix, adding it as a B-side to the single release of "Hangin' Tough." Ultimately, "Didn't I (Blow Your Mind)" ended up finding its way to the No. 8 spot on the *Billboard Top 200* chart and the *New Kids On The Block* album went on to sell 1 million copies by the end of 1989. It was later certified triple platinum by the RIAA.

By 1990, *Hangin' Tough* was flying off the shelves internationally and netted the band their first American Music Awards and Grammy Awards, helped by the award-winning docu-style VHS tape *New Kids On The Block: Hangin' Tough* (also done by director Doug Nichol). It came out in 1989 and gave a closer look into the band and their rise.

ABOVE: "You Got It (The Right Stuff)" single.

LEFT: NKOTB joy-riding in 1989.

Doug was there firsthand to see the shift as New Kids On The Block became the biggest band by the end of the '80s. "The first video I made was 'Please Don't Go Girl,' and they were just five kids and nobody noticed us on the street," he told *Variety*. "By the time I directed 'Hangin' Tough,' there were bodyguards and a mass of screaming, crying girls. Each time I came back to work with them, the fanbase was bigger and bigger. It was a touch of what Beatlemania must have been like, with crazy fans trying to get to these guys."

In March 2019, New Kids On The Block celebrated the thirtieth anniversary of *Hangin' Tough*, releasing a deluxe new edition with remixed songs and three additional tracks that weren't on the original in 1988, including "The Way," "Boys In The Band (Boy Band Anthem)," and "80s Baby," the latter featuring guest spots from contemporaries Debbie Gibson, Tiffany, Naughty By Nature, and Salt-N-Pepa.

Hangin' Tough would go on to place at No. 88 on *Billboard*'s 200 Greatest Albums of All Time list. In 1989, Maurice was named *Billboard*'s Songwriter of the Year, in large part due to the hits he churned out for his self-assembled boy band. And on April 24, 1989, the official New Kids On The Block Day was established by the Commonwealth of Massachusetts by then-governor Michael Dukakis, which all but put New Kids in the history books.

WHAT THE CRITICS SAID:
HANGIN' TOUGH

Not only did New Kids On The Block gain a lot of commercial fans with the release of their second album, they also gained the approval of critics, as seen in some of the reviews and recaps that have been written about *Hangin' Tough*. Of course, there were also the naysayers, a polarizing dynamic that would follow them the entirety of their career.

"'Hangin' Tough' isn't dangerous, and it never has been. It doesn't even try to be dangerous. Instead, it does its best to project a certain wild-boy energy. That gives the song a daffiness that I find slightly endearing. In a lot of ways, 'Hangin' Tough' sounds like an attempt to update chanty '70s bubblegum for a new jack swing era; it shares plenty of DNA, for instance, with something like the Bay City Rollers' 'Saturday Night.'"

—Tom Breihan, *Stereogum*

"*Hangin' Tough* [is] an infectious if derivative collection of street-smart dance pop and soulful crooning."

—David Wild, *Rolling Stone*

"[The album is} packed full of delectable pop singles of all shades, from the rebellious singalong title track to the peppy time capsule 'You Got It (The Right Stuff)' to the delicate and underrated R&B ballad that introduced them, 'Please Don't Go Girl.' Perhaps not a classic, but certainly a slice of compelling '80s pop music."

—Jason Thurston, *AllMusic*

"At 5 million and counting, this isn't the rank offense its demographic tilt would lead you to expect—auteur Maurice Starr has positioned two exceedingly cute uptempo hits atop two overly balladic sides. Really, why shouldn't a Black Svengali mastermind the safe white R&B ripoff for once? Funkier than The Osmonds or Milli Vanilli. As hip as New Edition."

—Robert Christgau, *Consumer Guide*

"An anniversary reissue of the New Kids' hit album affirms it as one of the better pure pop records of the late '80s."

—Maura Johnston, *The Boston Globe*

"We went on tour with Tiffany, and I remember coming home and it was like, 'Wow, it's different. We're famous. You have to act a little different now.' Not in a bad way, but I couldn't just run around the streets or go to a mall anymore."

—Jordan speaking to *Variety* in 2019

Danny poses with Halle Berry backstage during a circa 1989 concert.

CHAPTER EIGHT

HITTING THE ROAD

In the middle of *Hangin' Tough*'s two-year promo cycle, a serendipitous opportunity once again came knocking for New Kids On The Block: They booked their first tour. As the story goes, the New Kids were fans of it girl of the moment, Tiffany, who had a huge hit on her hands with a take on "I Think We're Alone Now," and the five teens went to see her perform in April 1988 at the Westbury Music Fair on Long Island, New York.

The New Kids had just signed to the same booking agent as Tiffany and were invited to go backstage to meet her. In a matter of right place, right time, Donnie, Danny, Jordan, Jonathan, and Joey entered her dressing room just as Tiffany was trying to figure out an opener for the show, and the boy band saved the day. NKOTB had a boombox with them backstage, and when Tiffany asked for them to play a song, she was so impressed with their talents and how good-looking they were that she asked them on the spot if they wanted the gig.

"I got in a lot of trouble with my manager. It was the first decision I ever made on my own and I got the phone call, like, 'You never do this! What are you doing?'" Tiffany explained to SiriusXM in 2019, during a panel conversation with NKOTB ahead of a reunion on that year's MixTape Tour. Proud of being the one to give the young talents their first shot, she conceded, "I know I did a really good thing. I've been so proud of these guys over the years."

When that very first gig at Westbury Music Fair became a smashing success, the offer was

A concert shot from the early 1990s.

extended for the New Kids to join Tiffany on her upcoming summer 1988 tour that included stops at a number of arenas and several Six Flags theme parks across the US, not to mention shopping malls (ground zero for the targeted teen fanbase).

Maurice got to work assembling a live band that could join New Kids On The Block on the road (as opposed to their earliest shows, in which they played to backing tracks); the original ensemble included musical director/ keyboardist Greg McPherson (who would soon become a thorn in the side of NKOTB), bassist David Dyson, keyboardist Yasko Kubota, guitarist Nerida Rojas, and drummer Derrick Antunes.

On the night of July 19, 1988, the musicians, crew, the teens—several of whom were fresh off high school graduation (Joey was still just fifteen years old)—and their parents met up at Maurice's house where a tour bus was waiting. The parents had put together "care packages"

the band could take with them in case they got homesick. Marlene Putnam, Jordan and Jonathan's mother, recalled to *People* that shortly after they headed out on the road, "They'd call home discouraged at first. 'The bus broke down; the air-conditioning doesn't work.' But as time went on, the calls home became more excited: 'You can't imagine! They love us out here!' The boys were so surprised."

Sure enough, the attention they got from fans—and lots and lots of girls—soon put any worries of loneliness to rest. A *Rolling Stone* profile in 1989 started with some color commentary on the "squealing young fans" waiting for the teen heartthrobs outside a hometown gig at the Worcester Arena.

It was also around this time that Tiffany and Jonathan became a teen fling, though it was very much shrouded. As NKOTB grew in fame, they were advised not to have girlfriends, to avoid breaking the hearts of their increasingly obsessive fanbase. The young couple dated for two years, but at the end of it, Jonathan was starting to come to terms with his true sexual identity and he broke things off with the pop star. They've remained friends ever since (even after she accidentally outed him in 2011).

Even with the growing fandom, the members of NKOTB were still normal teens and young adults—the *Rolling Stone* interview takes place while the quartet is sitting around the bus throwing a teddy bear back and forth; Danny had just worked out at a hotel gym; Joey's tutor is around. A *People* magazine article around the same time shares a setting where the New Kids are playing Nintendo and eating pizza.

This air of innocence was also a huge part of the band's success. As the *Tampa Bay Times* put it, the New Kids may have been "the first pop group to earn the *Good Housekeeping* Seal of Approval." As drug wars and AIDS ravaged American news cycles, and rap and heavy metal "devil's music" were taking over the airwaves, parents saw the New Kids as wholesome and representing good values (their name alone conjures up a Norman Rockwell painting). Parents deemed the New Kids as good role models and all but encouraged their kids to tune in, shelling out hard-earned money to take the whole family to shows in the late '80s and early '90s.

In fact, it's been reported that the New Kids tour rider stipulated that each show had to have a hospitality suite for parents of their young fanbase "and also asked that coffee and donuts be served to parents for free or at a minimal charge," says *Songfacts*. The *Rolling Stone* writer also came into contact with "hundreds of moms" that joined their young daughters "during all-night vigils that [became] standard procedure at the hotels where the Kids stay."

All of that came to a fever pitch in 1989 as NKOTB quickly embarked on their second tour. The story goes that, in late 1988, Tiffany and her team once again called on New Kids On The Block to be her opening act for her tour scheduled for summer 1989, in support of her new release, *Hold An Old Friend's Hand*.

They agreed—but a curious thing happened in the subsequent half-year before the tour

LEFT: Jonathan and Jordan with their mom, Marlene Putnam, in 1988.

RIGHT: Jordan (left) and Jonathan (right) with Tiffany, circa 1989.

ANOTHER STAR IS BORN

In much the same way as Tiffany gave New Kids On The Block their first big shot with the chance to open for her, NKOTB repaid the favor for none other than Lady Gaga (below, in 2008). When the Fab Five reunited in 2008, they gave the burgeoning "Poker Face" star the chance to support them on the road during their first tour in fourteen years. Lady Gaga had just released her debut album, *The Fame*, that August, but she was far from a household name yet. The tour with NKOTB marked her first arena gigs and her first time opening for a major act.

"Twenty years later [after touring with Tiffany], Lady Gaga opened for us and nobody knew her from Adam. She'd pop up in the studio and write with us and sing with us, and by the time the tour was over, we could've been her opening act," Donnie told SiriusXM in 2019.

It was actually Donnie who extended the invite after seeing Gaga a year prior as she dazzled in a performance of "Just Dance" at a Fourth of July bash in Vegas hosted by celebrity blogger Perez Hilton. Joey recalled to *Variety* that everyone in NKOTB could sense she was going to be a big star even back then, while Jordan remembered Gaga would make her own tour clothes and come to the band seeking their feedback.

Lady Gaga joined the tour on October 8, 2008, opening twenty-seven dates, ending on December 4. In the middle of it all, she also booked several solo club dates in order to make money for all the props and costumes that went over the budget allotted to her by her label, Interscope Records.

Those studio sessions Donnie referred to resulted in Lady Gaga appearing on New Kids On The Block's 2008 comeback album, *The Block*, for a song called "Big Girl Now," which she would often perform with them live while on the tour. The pop star also helped the band co-write the song, "Full Service."

began. New Kids On The Block had their first No. 1 hit with "I'll Be Loving You (Forever)," released in April 1989, and their fast-growing track to stardom actually led the booking agent to switch things up and have NKOTB close each show with Tiffany opening (though they were billed as co-headliners).

In a *Chicago Tribune* review of the concert on July 25, 1989, at Poplar Creek, journalist

Mark Caro wrote, "The headliner, according to the ticket, was Tiffany, but the crowd hadn't come for her. They came to scream their lungs out at those heartthrob teeny funkers, New Kids On The Block, who closed the show." Caro described the show as being more of a "pep rally" than a formal concert, noting, "The girls waved signs such as 'I (heart) (name of favorite New Kid On The Block)' and 'We're

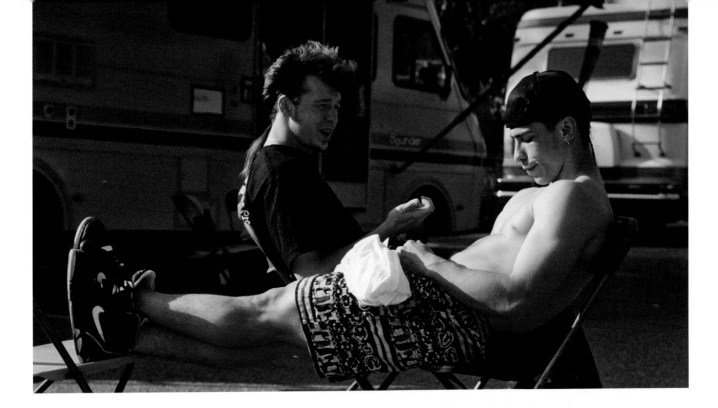

Available.'" Caro further criticized NKOTB's "overly rehearsed shtick" and "mastery of the Rock 'n' Roll Cliché Encyclopedia," though he also added, "The Kids were effective showmen, covering the stage with their choreographed hop-skip-and-jump dancing."

A *Los Angeles Times* article in June 1989 covering a show at the Celebrity Theatre in Anaheim also commented on the band's "shtick," with journalist Chris Willman saying, "the not-so-tightly scripted between-song shtick grew increasingly belabored and unbearable" and called their songs "mindless dance ditties," though the writer also commented on the mass throngs of teenage girls that didn't seem to mind but were rather "caught up in a frenzied kind of puppy love."

That puppy love translated into huge sales of merch. *Rolling Stone* estimated that the net was $100,000 for each performance on that 1989 tour, "or $15 per audience member." By tour dates in 1990, that figure basically doubled, according to the *Tampa Bay Times*,

who reported on thieves making away with all $260,000 that the New Kids made at one show in Montreal.

Another interesting thing happened by 1990. As Tiffany's career fell into a slump after her "I Think We're Alone Now" blitz, she cut ties with her original manager George Tobin and recruited none other than Maurice Starr to help revive her career.

ABOVE: New Kids fans react to catching a glimpse of the guys in Dorchester in 1990.

TOP: Donnie and Danny relax before a show, circa 1989.

"My holiday message is to think of Christmas as a time of giving instead of getting. To think of people less fortunate than us . . . to be a loving person."

—Jordan sharing his thoughts on Christmas with fans in a 1989 video message

New Kids On The Block on the *New York Daily News* float at the Macy's Thanksgiving Day Parade in 1989.

CHAPTER NINE

SEASON'S GREETINGS

After years of hard work and persistence, New Kids On The Block had one more gift before the 1980s wrapped up, releasing a Christmas album in September 1989, on the brink of their commercial peak. It would be their one and only holiday album to date and was full of seasonal covers as well as original songs. It was whipped together in record time while the band was on tour, with many of the songs recorded in hotel rooms while on the road. Among the familiar holiday picks on NKOTB's *Merry, Merry Christmas* were covers of Irving Berlin's "White Christmas," "The Little Drummer Boy," and "The Christmas Song" (aka "Chestnuts Roasting on an Open Fire").

Maurice Starr teamed up with composer/producer Al Lancellotti to help pen a few originals as well, including "Last Night I Saw Santa Claus," "I Still Believe in Santa Claus," and the title track, while singer-songwriter Kenny Nolan assisted on "I'll Be Missing You Come Christmas (A Letter to Santa)." Maurice also worked with Donnie to write "Funky, Funky Xmas," though Maurice's giant contribution was the song "This One's For The Children," which became the defining track of the album. It headed to No. 7 on the *Billboard* Hot 100 chart in December of that year and helped the album sell a total of 2 million copies.

ABOVE: Joey performs with Lea Michele in 2017, during a taping of *The Wonderful World of Disney: Magical Holiday Celebration* at Disneyland in Anaheim, California.

TOP: The New Kids perform with the Backstreet Boys in Times Square on New Year's Eve 2011.

A quasi take on Band-Aid's "Do They Know It's Christmas?" NKOTB's "This One's For The Children" begins with the narration, "This is a very serious message, so all of you please listen," with lyrics about young ones all around the world facing hunger and a plea to help those in need, all padded by a religious tone.

The music video, with 10 million views and counting on YouTube, also tugs on the heart strings, showing images of young kids from every corner of the globe interspersed with clips of the band around a piano, clapping along to the song's beat as Jordan sings lead. Although much of the album is full of holiday cheese, *AllMusic* says, "'This One's for the Children' is a genuinely strong holiday song that deserved to be the Top 10 hit that it was."

There was a charitable mission to the song as well—New Kids On The Block donated proceeds from "This One's For The Children" to the United Cerebral Palsy organization and also appeared on UCP's telethon in 1989 to sing the hit song and help raise funds. It is a charity NKOTB would return to many times throughout their career, first linked through one of their managers, Dick Scott, who was an associate producer for the telethons, according to *Variety*. In addition to the Christmas song proceeds, money from the band's new 1-900 telephone number (where fans could call and hear personal message from the New Kids) was also donated heavily to UCP.

MORE GIFTS TO UNWRAP

Though New Kids On The Block only have one official Christmas album to their name, the group revisited the idea in 2017, when they included three new seasonal tracks on a deluxe edition of that year's EP, *Thankful*. The *Thankful, Unwrapped* version offered the festive songs "Unwrap You," "One Night of Peace," and "December Love."

Individual members have also recorded a number of holiday songs over the years. Jordan released "Little Drummer Boy" on his 2006 solo album *Love Songs*, while Joey's 2011 *Come Home For Christmas* solo album featured covers of eleven holiday staples, and some special guests to boot including his son, Griffin, and sister, Carol.

During the pandemic pause in 2020, New Kids On The Block hosted a special "holiday potluck" livestream for fans, allowing them to connect with their favorite band at the most wonderful time of the year. The idea continued a trend NKOTB started in the '90s, in which they recorded holiday messages that were broadcast out. During the potluck, which was hosted by their new manager Jared Paul, the five guys donned festive looks and were situated in front of holiday backdrops. Danny also introduced his new YouTube cooking channel, "The Wood Works," in which he shares his and his mom Betty's recipes and offered a filmed instructional for making his mom's famous holiday coffee cake.

A few televised opportunities happened around the holidays too. First came a "Christmas Special" of the New Kids' cartoon series in December 1990. IMDb describes the plot: "After a New York concert, Donnie finds a homeless kid who wants him to come to his mother's shelter home. The New Kids spread Christmas joy to those less fortunate." NKOTB also appeared on *Dick Clark's Rockin' Eve* program twice, the first time on December 31, 2010, as part of promotions for NKOTBSB, and then again as just the New Kids at the tail end of 2018.

And, of course, who could forget all the NKOTB holiday merch fans have gotten to unwrap year after year?

By the time New Year's Eve 1989 rolled around, New Kids On The Block were featured in several year-end roundups highlighting a yearbook of cultural phenomena from the year. *Entertainment Tonight* heralded, "It looks like Beatlemania 25 years later, but this time it's New Kids On The Block, creating the music industry's biggest sensation of 1989." The program added that movie, TV, and merchandise deals were in the works, setting the stage for a lucrative new year and new decade ahead.

The New Kids in concert, circa 1990.

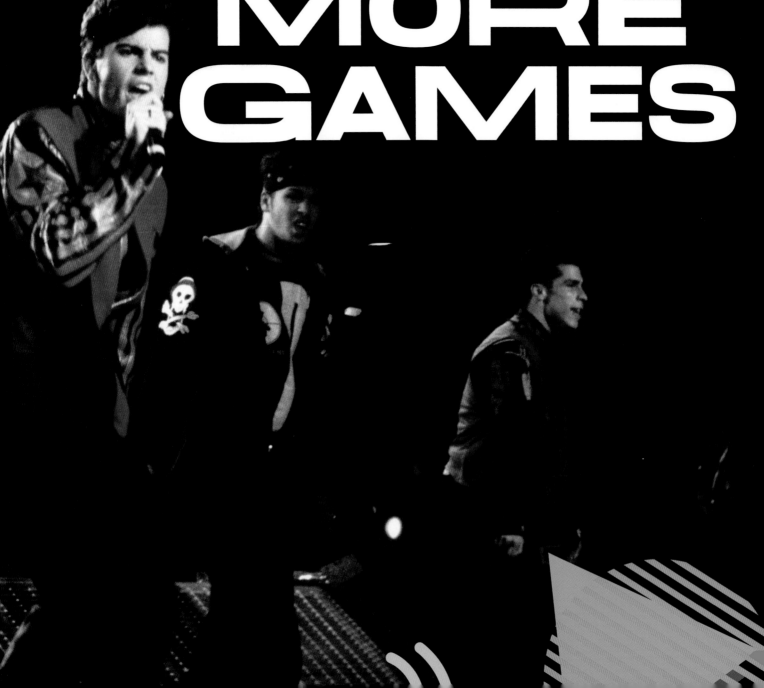

NO MORE GAMES

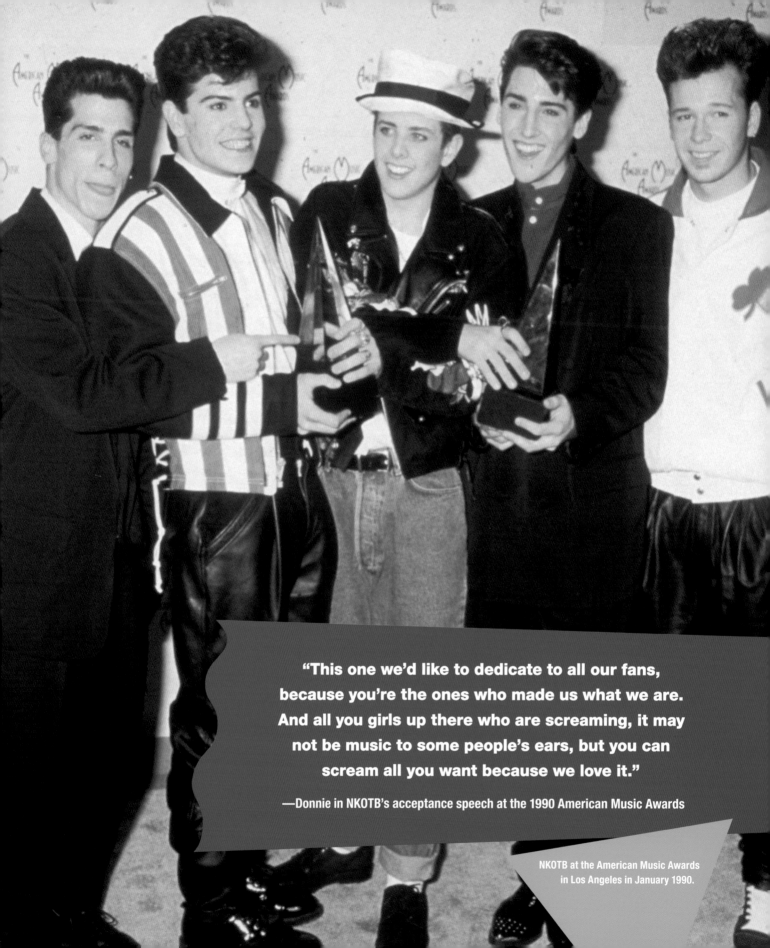

"This one we'd like to dedicate to all our fans, because you're the ones who made us what we are. And all you girls up there who are screaming, it may not be music to some people's ears, but you can scream all you want because we love it."

—Donnie in NKOTB's acceptance speech at the 1990 American Music Awards

NKOTB at the American Music Awards in Los Angeles in January 1990.

CHAPTER TEN

THE AWARDS START ROLLING IN

By the beginning of 1990, New Kids On The Block was widely regarded as "the most financially successful group in pop," as told by the *New York Times*, thanks to their unprecedented success over the previous year, including 15 million records sold. As the album sales started pouring in, naturally, awards soon followed. MTV nominated the band for a "best choreography" Video Music Award in 1989, and the Boston Music Awards heaped a number of accolades (eight total) on the group from 1989 to 1991.

But the crowning moment came on January 20, 1990, when NKOTB shocked everyone by bringing home a pair of wins at the American Music Awards, their first-ever national award show. Held at the Shrine Auditorium in Los Angeles, the 17th annual American Music Awards was broadcast on ABC for a huge at-home audience. It was hosted by Gloria Estefan, the Judds, and Anita Baker, and featured performances from, among others, Janet Jackson, Paula Abdul, Richard Marx, Warrant, and, of course, New Kids On The Block.

Introduced by Gloria, NKOTB took to the stage in a shroud of screams as they ran

Danny, Jonathan, Joey, Donnie, and Jordan pose during an interview, circa 1989.

through a seamless medley of their biggest hits from the year prior. They began the performance silhouetted on a red background and taking a pose while delivering the first few lines of "Cover Girl." It was quickly followed by "Hangin' Tough," as Donnie stepped forward (dressed in a leather jacket printed with a riff on the American flag) and delivered a monologue about the song's origins. "You know fellas, since our days back in Boston, there's been a lot of doors shut in our face, even 'til now. But we're gonna keep on 'hangin' tough,'" he said, leading the house in a massive clap-a-long. The band then moved into "You Got It (The Right Stuff)" and curiously added in their big Christmas hit, "This One's For The Children," to wrap it up.

When it came time to dole out the awards they were nominated for, it was quite the shock to most people in the room. For the award for Favorite Pop/Rock Duo or Group, presented by singer-songwriter Stephen Bishop and pop singer and *Grease* actress Olivia Newton-John, NKOTB was up against hair metal gods Bon Jovi and the pre-scandal Euro dance-pop phenom Milli Vanilli (who were the most award-winning act that night). The New Kids won. They were promptly booed by rows of (mostly) men in the crowd, while fan girls attempted to drown out the jeering. "I know we're making you guys real mad up there who are booing," Joey said upon stepping up to the mic to give the acceptance speech, "but I'm sorry, we're doing it for the girls up there." Donnie then promptly dedicated the award to NKOTB's fans, eliciting even louder cheering.

They were also given the award for Favorite Pop/Rock Album, besting both Paula Abdul (nominated for her groundbreaking debut *Forever Your Girl*) and none other than former New Edition member Bobby Brown, whose solo album *Don't Be Cruel* was the top-grossing record of 1989. "Not bad for five boys from Dorchester, huh?" Donnie shared, taking the mic stand as four of the five members walked up the stage to receive the award. Jonathan was notably missing; Joey tried to explain it away as he needed more time for their live performance—"he's still in the group, no rumors," Joey said—but, in the years since, it's been revealed Jonathan's debilitating anxiety crept up in this moment.

Donnie helped fill the stage by shining a spotlight on Maurice Starr and inviting their manager/producer to join them for the defining moment. "We want to bring up someone who's been called by many people many things, but he's never been anything to us but a very, very good friend. . . . Without him having his dream, we could've never had our dreams come true." The four embraced Maurice in a group huddle, and Donnie wrapped things up by giving a shout-out to the other nominees that had been included in the categories NKOTB won. He commended the artists "for helping us show that music truly is the international language and the universal language, even if it is spoken with a Boston accent."

If New Kids On The Block were trying to show they had something to prove to the big guns in the crowd—literally, Guns N' Roses were there—they did so that night. In a recap for the *Los Angeles Times*, writer Dennis Hunt called the whole broadcast a "fountain of youth" and likened it to "a teen version of the Grammys," where many of the winners—not the least of which was NKOTB—were highly prized by the youngest demographic.

As the writer pointed out, the American Music Awards are basically done by fan votes, and NKOTB's voracious fan base pushed hard for them with call-ins—and also showed up in person. As Dennis Hunt said, the New Kids were the clear favorite of the night, "mobbed by the fans who wandered around the fringes of the backstage area [and] . . . swarmed all over their limo when they arrived."

The NKOTB blitz showed no signs of slowing over the next twelve months—it would be the most prolific time for the band in terms of nominations and honorary titles. By the end of 1990, New Kids On The Block also won the award for the No. 1 Pop Group at the inaugural *Billboard* Music Awards, though they were unable to accept it in person due to their nonstop tour schedule that year.

Fans welcome home New Kids On The Block in Boston's South Station in July 1990.

THE MAN WITH THE VISION

One of the most important visionaries behind the early days of New Kids On The Block (besides Maurice Starr) was video director Doug Nichol (right), who all but helped the teens create their image and overall aesthetic. Before he made the music video for "Please Don't Go Girl" (using $9,000 of Maurice's own money), the world really only knew the New Kids by their voices on record and some still photos seen in the cover art and magazine spreads.

But with Doug's music videos—which included the important series of "Please Don't Go Girl," "I'll Be Loving You (Forever)," "You Got It (The Right Stuff)," "Hangin' Tough," and "This One's For The Children"—the five members became fully dimensional characters for fans to idolize.

Doug reunited with NKOTB at the band's first-ever BLOCKCON fan convention in 2023, where he sat on a panel discussing his concepts and some revealing behind-the-scenes moments. Among the tidbits was the fact that the band often did only one or two takes of a video, since film was so pricey at the time. Discussing "You Got It (The Right Stuff)," Doug recalled picking out a cemetery in New Orleans as the backdrop because he loved the movie *Easy Rider*. For the "I'll Be Loving You (Forever)" video, fans were starting to figure out where the guys would be and showed up for the filming, which helped with some last-minute casting.

But perhaps most interesting was Doug's story of flying to remote locations to film kids around the world for "This One's For The Children." When the crew got to Egypt, it was around the same time Libyan leader Muammar Gaddafi was paying a visit. The film crew was seen as an untrusted threat, so they were arrested and spent a night in jail.

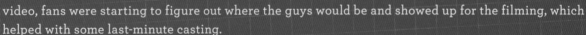

They also won big at the Dave Coulier-hosted Nickelodeon Kids' Choice Awards in April 1990, taking Favorite Male Musician/Group as well as Favorite Song for "Hangin' Tough" ("Step By Step" was also nominated in this category). In both categories, they were once again victorious over Bobby Brown, Bon Jovi, and Milli Vanilli. The New Kids' intense tour schedule prevented them from appearing on this broadcast, too, though they did send a pair of video acceptance speeches via satellite. Jordan and Donnie appeared in each one, holding Nickelodeon's famous blimp awards. For the Favorite Song award, Donnie even proceeded to do an improv rap about their win, commanding a roar of applause from the young crowd in attendance at the ceremony.

Although the New Kids themselves weren't nominated for the more high-brow Grammy Awards in 1990, a video done by their go-to visual guru Doug Nichol was. The docu-style *Hangin' Tough* was nominated in the "Best Music Video, Long Form" category, which was first established by the Recording Academy in 1984 and was meant to honor directors and performers for quality visual pieces. Doug and NKOTB (along with producer Bryan Johnson) were up against the Eurythmics' *Savage*, Michael Jackson's *Moonwalker*, Pink Floyd's *In Concert: Delicate Sound of Thunder*, and Janet Jackson's *Rhythm Nation 1814*, the latter of which ultimately won.

Yet the loss did nothing to deter interest as the thirty-minute film (which captured the end of NKOTB's 1989 tour alongside live footage and music videos) became one of the highest-grossing VHS tapes of all time. In 1990 alone, it sold 1.25 million copies, according to the *New York Times*, and would go on to gross record-breaking sales of $48 million, per *IMDb*.

As Doug told *Entertainment Tonight* in 2019, he had a go-to theme he often returned to with New Kids On The Block videos that always seemed to work: "[It] was always the vibe of their videos—the guys are hanging around, then they meet up with some girls and have a sweet, innocent time," he adds. "If you watch all of the videos, that's what happens!"

TOP: Jonathan poses during a circa 1989 video shoot.

BOTTOM: The New Kids sign autographs for fans in the late '80s or early '90s.

The New Kids in Florida in 1989.

"We were maybe the originators of doing things business-wise . . . with our fans."

—Danny in a video interview posted to his YouTube page in 2015

The New Kids take a soda break, circa 1989.

CHAPTER ELEVEN

MAD FOR MERCH

In the 1990s, it was hard to go *anywhere* without seeing the faces of the New Kids on magazines, food items, clothing, housewares, trinkets, and even dolls. The five boys from Boston were plucked from literal obscurity overnight to become the poster children for a merchandising dynasty.

The idea was no doubt planted after the team behind NKOTB saw how many units their "hastily assembled" novelty holiday album, *Merry, Merry Christmas*, sold at the end of 1989. As *Grammy.com* shared, the holiday album's popularity "exemplified fans' determination to get their hands on anything NKOTB—and the industry's determination to capitalize on this." Soon after, said the outlet, "you couldn't do your weekly shopping without seeing the boys' idolized faces staring back at you, whether on a magazine front cover, official doll, or Coca-Cola ad campaign."

There was money to be made off New Kids On The Block—and the numbers were staggering. As mentioned, concert revenues topped $100,000 per night in 1989 (*New York Times* actually says it was closer to $125,000); by 1990, that figure had more than doubled to $260,000 (at least at the Montreal show, when thieves made off with the proceeds). And that was just concerts. *People* estimated that, by the end of 1990, the New Kids would have grossed $400 million from lucrative merchandising deals.

It was all the handiwork of Dell Furano, dubbed the "king of merch" in an obituary posted to *Pollstar* upon his death in 2021. Dell made groundbreaking moves when it came to launching and re-assessing the potential of marketed products for musical artists. He began his career with the other fan-centric behemoth the Grateful Dead in the 1970s and then extrapolated the possibilities with KISS' mega-licensing deals shortly thereafter. It was in the '80s, however, that Dell really found his footing, steering the product lines of acts like Madonna, Michael Jackson, Bruce Springsteen (making his 1984 tour the biggest grossing in concert merch ever), and of course, New Kids On The Block.

In a 2016 interview posted to Epic Rights—the multi-layered artist services company he owned with his wife Kym—Dell explained how things shifted in the '80s, right around the time that NKOTB presented a prime opportunity. "In the beginning, we only sold merch at concerts. By the mid-'80s, we started selling and licensing others to sell—record stores, head

The New Kids, and some even newer Kids (doll versions of themselves).

shops, jean shops, followed by selling to major retailers and ultimately direct online."

Dell further explained that a deal with New Kids On The Block was first struck in 1987, after their beleaguered debut album flop but just on the precipice of *Hangin' Tough*'s success—and retail became the main economic driver. "We licensed every product imaginable: Dolls, sneakers, stationery products, apparel, jewelry, McDonald's Happy Meals, books, board games, posters, caps, sunglasses, animated TV series, stand ups, etc."

In an interview with *Billboard* in 2017, Dell expounded on the significance of NKOTB's merchandising and licensing deals, hailing the band as a "watershed artist" showing the incredible potential for feeding the fans every

piece of memorabilia they could possibly want—and then some. New Kids marked the "first huge blowout by a boy band at retail," said Dell, even recalling making moves with department store JCPenney, in which Donnie, Danny, Jordan, Jonathan, and Joey's family members went on their *own* tour to host events in store locations around the US.

The success was so remarkable that New Kids made four times the amount of money on merchandise as they did on their own music. The *Tampa Bay Times*, citing the *Wall Street Journal*, reported that a whopping "80% of the New Kids take comes from merchandising, 15% from record sales, and 5% from concerts."

As the New Kids' fame peaked in the very late '80s/early '90s, there was an "all-in" mentality by the band's team, too, probably knowing the allure of the boy band wouldn't live on forever. Fans would get older, and much like the Barbies and Tonkas they'd toss aside, so would go the New Kids product potpourri. As the *Tampa Bay Times* reported in August 1990, even back then, "The unofficial buzz among high schoolers is that to be 16 or 17 and still have New Kids posters on the wall is woefully out of step." (Though tell that to the tens of thousands of fans who tipped the scales for New Kids On The Block again in 2019, as their Mixtape Tour brought in more than $50 million, as reported by *Billboard*. In 2022, New Kids signed on with Epic Rights to establish a new worldwide merchandise program.)

The potential fleeting moments didn't seem to faze the band or their team. As manager Dick Scott told *People*, "If it's over tomorrow, so what? Today we're the biggest group in the world." In a press conference to launch their line of Hasbro action figures, Donnie also commented on the temporality questions:

ABOVE: Dell Furano (right) and his wife, Kym, in 2014.

LEFT: Just some of the merch collected by a fan over the decades.

"Everyone is so concerned about the future of New Kids On The Block and this and that, and whether we're going to be 'old men on the block.' We're just having a ball now and that's all we're really worried about."

TOP: The New Kids get animated.

BOTTOM: A Blockhead shows off their NKOTB jacket at a Boston concert in July 1990.

It wasn't just physical products that the New Kids shelled out in droves to fans, either. Some of the other ingenious ideas included a short-lived animated series (developed by DIC Entertainment) that aired on Saturday mornings on ABC for one season in 1990. (The Disney Channel ran reruns from 1991 to 1993.) *New Kids On The Block*, the TV show, turned Donnie, Danny, Jonathan, Jordan, and Joey into cartoon characters who got into mischief while on the road; even Maurice was a character. The episodes, of course, featured the New Kids' music (including concert footage for scene transitions), and the real-life members appeared as themselves to introduce episodes or foreshadow the "lesson" to come.

Perhaps the best marketing ploy of all, though, was the 1-900 hotline that fans could call into (1-900-909-5KIDS, to be exact). Back in the days of landlines, kids would

LEAVE A MESSAGE AFTER THE BEEP. . .

I n case it's been a minute since you called up 900-909-5KIDS, here's a sampling of what you might have heard on the New Kids hotline, as relayed by the Washington Post in 1990:

"Push 1 if you'd like to listen in on the New Kids' talking bulletin board."

"Push 2 if you'd like to record your personal message for Jordan, Jon, Donnie, Danny, Joe, or other fans nationwide."

"Push 3 to let the New Kids know what songs you'd like them to do live in your town this summer on the Magic Summer Tour, where they'll be singing some new songs from their brand-new album titled *Step By Step*."

"Push 4 if you'd like to hear the New Kids On The Block Magic Summer Tour schedule."

"Push 5 if you'd like to hear samples from the New Kids' first two albums: the multi-platinum-selling *Hangin' Tough* and the original New Kids' album featuring the smash hit, 'Didn't I Blow Your Mind.'"

"Push 6 if you'd like to receive a free personalized fan club letter and packet from the New Kids On The Block."

"Push 7 if you'd like to hear about the special offerings and savings on New Kids On The Block merchandise and how you can place an order right now."

tie up their parents' rotary just to get some time with the Kids—the hotline provided the chance to hear the latest news, sit in on New Kids' conversations, listen to other fans gush about the band, or even leave the Fab Five messages. "Now you can hang tough with us 24 hours a day on our brand-new hotline," said Donnie in a commercial. Of course, the pitch was followed by a narrator telling kids to "get your parents' permission first"—especially since they'd be the ones footing the bill for $2 for the first minute and 45 cents for every minute thereafter. (A portion of sales did

benefit NKOTB's favorite charity organization, United Cerebral Palsy, at least.)

The *Washington Post* reports that 4.5 million calls were placed in a one-year span between 1989 (when the hotline was first established) and 1990; *CBS This Morning* stated it was bringing in $500,000-plus a month. Even pop star Pink was once a frequent caller. As she revealed on *The Tonight Show Starring Jimmy Fallon* in 2015, she racked up a $118 phone bill and was promptly grounded. "I talked to all of them—all the time," she shared. "We were practically getting married."

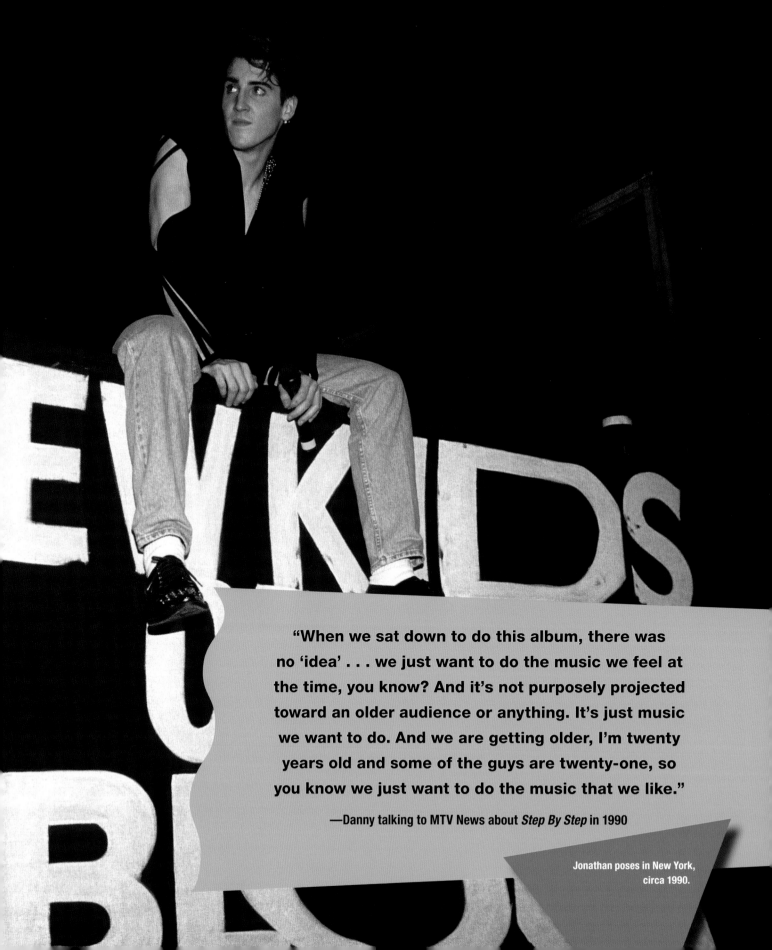

"When we sat down to do this album, there was no 'idea' . . . we just want to do the music we feel at the time, you know? And it's not purposely projected toward an older audience or anything. It's just music we want to do. And we are getting older, I'm twenty years old and some of the guys are twenty-one, so you know we just want to do the music that we like."

—Danny talking to MTV News about *Step By Step* in 1990

Jonathan poses in New York, circa 1990.

CHAPTER TWELVE

MOVING FORWARD WITH STEP BY STEP

Capitalizing on their newfound demigod status, New Kids On The Block wasted no time in taking giant leaps towards their next album. Work on *Step By Step* started in September 1989, and the record was released on June 5, 1990, just nine months after *Merry, Merry Christmas* and less than two years after 1988's *Hangin' Tough*. Demand was so intense for the album (with 2 million pre-orders placed) that, as reported by the *New York Times*, "The demand put [Columbia's] pressing plants into overtime production."

The album's first single, the super-catchy title track, was released May 10, 1990, and became an instant, massive hit: "Step By Step" sold 1 million copies by that July and remained at the top of the *Billboard* charts for three consecutive weeks. The song notably features all five New Kids on lead vocals at one point

or another within the four-and-a-half-minute track—but it wasn't even intended to be a NKOTB song at all.

Maurice Starr originally wrote "Step By Step" in 1987, and it was recorded by Boston R&B group the Superiors and distributed via Motown Records. The Superiors' recording barely made

The New Kids take a break in Chicago in 1990.

a blip; yet New Kids found their biggest-selling single. It also remains their most-loved song, evidenced by the 68 million and counting spins on Spotify; that's 14 million ahead of their next most-favored track, "I'll Be Loving You (Forever)." The music video for "Step By Step" also has 63 million views as of publication date, the infamous reel showing the New Kids engaging in fancy synchronized footwork and high jumps that showcased their incredible dexterity and hallmark dedication to choreography.

Other singles from *Step By Step* included "Valentine Girl," released in June 1990; "Tonight," released in July; and "Let's Try It Again," the final entrant, which came out in September. Like *Hangin' Tough*, nearly each single was accompanied by a music video (sans "Let's Try It Again") and another direct-to-

VHS, long-form home video was released that became a blockbuster hit.

Step By Step the docu-video had preorders of 500,000 units, "the largest initial shipment of videos [CBS Music Videos] had ever made" back then, according to the *New York Times*. It was certified gold by the Recording Industry Association of America® in August 1990, following the success of the *Hangin' Tough* and *Hangin' Tough Live* tapes that sold more than 2.2 million copies.

Like the other three NKOTB albums to date, most of the songwriting was done by Maurice, who by then was gaining a reputation as a mastermind. "Maurice has his finger on the pulse of teen America," Don Ienner, president of Columbia Records, told *Entertainment Weekly*. The *South Florida Sun-Sentinel* brandished

Maurice as "the biggest guy in pop music, the newest tycoon of teen. He's the next Berry Gordy, the next Phil Spector, the next Quincy Jones, the new P.T. Barnum."

But there were a couple songs where he was more hands-off. One was the quirky funk pop track "Games," written by Donnie, with some quintessential rap verses and a chorus riffing on the chant of the Wicked Witch's foot soldiers in *The Wizard Of Oz*. The other was album closer "Never Gonna Fall In Love Again," scribed by Danny in conjunction with TaharQa and Tunde Ra Aleem, the twin brother duo known for working with Jimi Hendrix and for founding NIA Records, which kickstarted the career of none other than the Wu-Tang Clan.

But, unlike *Hangin' Tough*, the band wasn't wholly confined to Maurice's studio shack at the House of Hits to make *Step By Step*. They also logged recording time between September 1989 to April 1990 in more professional settings, including Mission Control in Westford, Massachusetts; the Hit Cave in Brookline, Massachusetts; Normandy Recording Studio in Warren, Rhode Island; and Syncro Sound in Boston.

In a video promo for *Step By Step*, Donnie said the album name was an "accurate one, because all along that's sort of how we felt. When we talk about our music, and the way we try to express ourselves through music, we've only taken it one step at a time, step by step. We're doing the music we feel now in 1990, that's what we want to get out there."

Danny expanded on that sentiment, saying the album name symbolized the band taking "steps up musically," and adding, "I feel this is the next step up for us to take with this album."

There is a lot to be said of the stylistic detours New Kids took with *Step By Step*,

experimenting more with hip-hop that was prevalent at the time (Donnie wears a Public Enemy T-shirt in the title track's music video), but also funk and reggae and adding full string sections to certain songs. "Tonight" was even hailed as the closest the band could get to Paul McCartney's sheen. In the promo video, the five members are also seen playing many of the instruments. Ultimately, *Stereogum* noted that the song "Step By Step" set a boy band precedent: "Nobody had mastered the boy-band art of trading off lead vocals within every song; that wouldn't happen until the late '90s."

"It's still our style of music," Jordan said in the promotional piece, "but we got a chance to show our singing ability a lot more. And the production is so much better—all the strings are real. Every album we did was a step up and this was definitely a step up from *Hangin' Tough*."

The promo video ends with a chorus of screaming fan girls trying to rush a backstage door, a familiar sight for New Kids On The Block in the early '90s. Wherever NKOTB went, an eruption of shrieking followed.

Step by Step
on vinyl.

British New Kids fans gather before a concert in April 1990.

The screaming happened nearly every night on tour—so much so that *Washington Post* ended their concert preview with a P.S. to parents: "If you're accompanying your children to Wednesday's show, bring earplugs. We're not kidding. Even if you're going to be sitting in your car in the parking lot, it might not be a bad idea. It's not for the music: A critic who's seen the New Kids in Baltimore and at Capital Centre says the sound of nearly 50,000 shrilling little girls will push you way beyond the threshold of pain."

The shrill howls also happened during countless TV appearances as the New Kids did a mega PR blitz for *Step By Step*. You couldn't even hear Oprah Winfrey when she hosted the boy band on a November 1990 episode. On *Good Morning America*, host Chantal Westerman shared, "They're screaming from the top of their lungs to the bottom of their hearts," trying to find some kind of poetic prose to offset the all-out hysteria in her live shots.

There was even a near-riot in New York City, when the New Kids headed to the Hard Rock Café to introduce their new Hasbro dolls in February 1990. "They may be New Kids On The Block, but they're old enough to create mass hysteria," began a news broadcast on NYC's WPIX, showing hundreds of shrieking girls and an assembly of cops trying to hold them back. "The cops were grabbing at everybody," said one fan in the newscast; "I was almost killed but it was worth it," another shared.

Countless opinion pieces at the time compared the New Kids blitzkrieg to Beatlemania—but there were also hints the peak of the band's fame was starting to crest. MTV's John Norris said as much as he introduced an interview with the band in 1990 and pressed Donnie on rumors that he was planning to leave the group. "There's so much stuff in all the tabloids . . . a lot of people are going to believe a lot of stuff that they hear but no it's not true. I don't have any plans on going anywhere," Donnie rebutted.

Still, the downward-tracking sales spiral of *Step By Step* was another indicator something may have been amiss. Though the title track stayed on top of the *Billboard* charts for three weeks, from May to June 1990, "Tonight" only entered at No. 7, and by the time "Let's Try It Again" was released in November, it didn't even make a dent in the Top 50 (it entered at No. 53). In total, *Step By Step* sold 3 million copies. Though significant, it paled in comparison to the 7 million units moved for *Hangin' Tough* in a year's time.

Yet, there was the undeniable draw of the Magic Summer/No More Games Tour—a grueling 220-date, two-year international trek—that kept New Kids On The Block top of mind through early 1992, and made them some of the richest people in America.

WHAT THE CRITICS SAID:
STEP BY STEP

As New Kids On The Block released their next commercial success with *Step By Step*, they still struggled to get wide critical acclaim and rise above boy band status. In fact, they were named 1989's "worst band" by *Rolling Stone* and their readers. A look at some of the critical reviews of *Step By Step* shows the great divide.

"*Step By Step* is a deeply messy and slapdash album. Even though it's the much-hyped *Hangin' Tough* follow-up, it plays like a quickie cash-grab, not too different from the Christmas record that preceded it."

—Tom Breihan, *Stereogum*

"[A] slick compendium of pop styles, from doo-wop to hip-hop, is the group's most musically sophisticated album and a sure-fire blockbuster."

—Stephen Holden, *New York Times*

"Someone ought to tell the New Kids they can't adopt new musical styles quite as easily as they throw on new outfits. But then it's not important what anyone tells them. . . . Two million copies of this album have been shipped, which means it can already claim multiplatinum status. Maybe soon it will be certified uranium, if the music industry cares to honor the New Kids by contriving a still more exalted mega-measure of a record's success. It makes no difference—not in any way that affects record sales—that most of the songs are notable mainly for their commercial sheen."

—Greg Sandow, *Entertainment Weekly*

"*Step by Step* does sport a feistier version of the Kids, even while it largely sticks to their set musical formula and entirely to their chosen image. Donnie Wahlberg, Jon Knight, Joe McIntyre, Danny Wood, and Jordan Knight each get turns singing lead, thanks to the group's determination to present itself as a unit and the commercial demands of its crucial live shows; more than one fan would leave Kids concerts brokenhearted if her favorite wasn't given equal time at the mic. . . . Have the New Kids come into their own? Probably, although they didn't have far to go. The Kids weren't as immature in the first place as their critics thought, and they're not as mature as they think they are now. But no twelve-year-old girl cares."

—Arion Berger, *Rolling Stone*

New Kids on tour, circa 1990.

"On the road, I can't even go out in the hallway of a hotel. Some days it gets to me pretty bad. If I want to go out at night, I go to a punk club where they don't care who I am."

—Jordan speaking to *People* in 1990

The New Kids perform in Paris in 1991.

CHAPTER THIRTEEN

THE NEVER-ENDING TOUR

Any notion that interest was waning for New Kids On The Block was squashed by the record-breaking success of the Magic Summer Tour. Kicking off in April 1990 and running through February 1992 (the latter half rebranded as the No More Games Tour), the 220-date, four-continent trek was an unparalleled road log and, as *Rolling Stone* once put it, "exhibit[ed] a marked unwillingness to go away."

To understand how huge the tour was, simply consider the records NKOTB broke. In 1990 alone, the tour garnered $74 million in ticket sales, making the band the "top-grossing touring act" of the year, according to the *Los Angeles Times*. The New Kids were well ahead of the runner-up act, Billy Joel, who raked in $43 million, and NKOTB did nearly double what Paul McCartney was able to accomplish that year with $37 million in ticket sales. They also left Janet Jackson and M.C. Hammer in the dust, who grossed a respective $28.2 million and $26.3 million. Even fellow Bostonites Aerosmith fell behind, with a paltry $27.4 million. New Kids' combined 3.29 million concert tickets also bested the Rolling Stones, who sold 3.25 million.

In return, it made New Kids On The Block some of the richest people in America. By 1991, *Forbes* put NKOTB at the top of their list

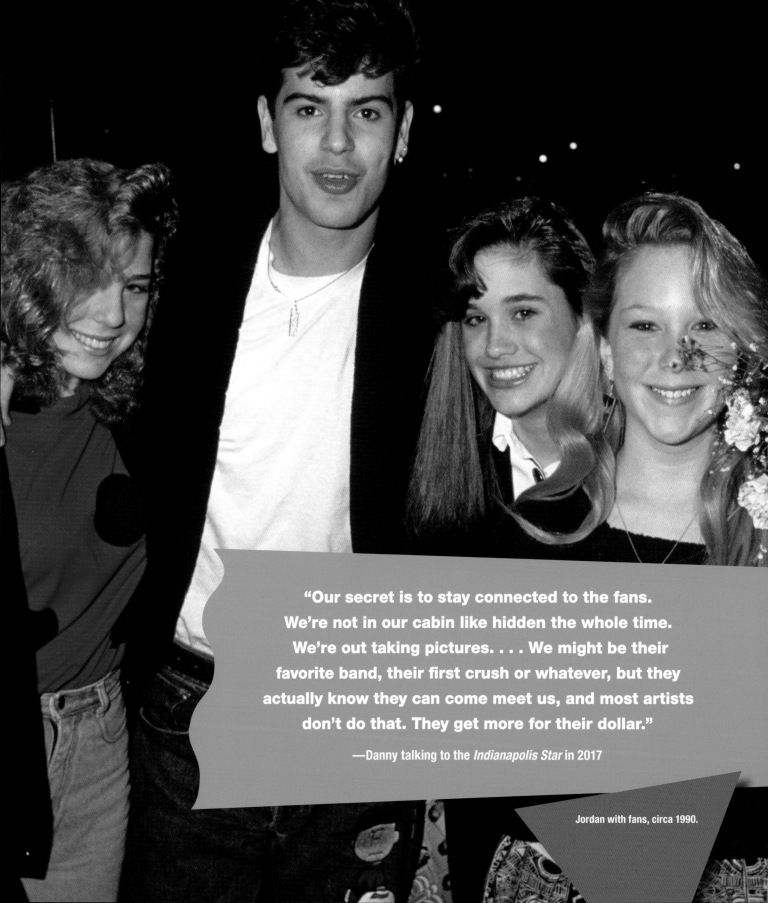

"Our secret is to stay connected to the fans. We're not in our cabin like hidden the whole time. We're out taking pictures. . . . We might be their favorite band, their first crush or whatever, but they actually know they can come meet us, and most artists don't do that. They get more for their dollar."

—Danny talking to the *Indianapolis Star* in 2017

Jordan with fans, circa 1990.

CHAPTER FOURTEEN

BLOCK NATION AND THE BLOCKHEADS

They call themselves Blockheads, and they continue to be one of the most voracious and engaged band fan clubs of all time. Not only did the fans contribute to NKOTB reaching a $1 billion merchandise benchmark by 1991, but they also signed up in droves for the official fan club. In the '90s, the *New York Times* estimated that membership totaled about 100,000 people, while the group's special fan-focused 900-number was bringing in, on average, 400,000 calls a month.

In the beginning, the New Kids' own mothers ran the fan club operation from an official headquarters in Boston (it's here that you could write to them, addressed to P.O. Box 7080, Quincy, MA 02269). While the parents weren't paid, per say, all of the New Kids bought their parents new homes as their bank accounts fattened up.

The fan club HQ handled anywhere from 20,000 to 40,000 letters every week in the late '80s and early '90s, according to the *Daily Press*. "They're screened first by the moms of the band members," Howard Tyner, then fan club marketing director, told the newspaper. "They respond to most of them and pass them on to the Kids."

Canadian fans await their chance to buy NKOTB tickets in Toronto in October 1990.

If you signed up for a NKOTB fan club membership back then, it cost $18 a year and you were given an official card with a photo of the five guys on the front and your fan club number on the back, plus a pin declaring you to be an "official member," and a badge you could sew onto your jean jacket. Every so often, a personal care package would arrive in the mail—sometimes it included glossy photos of the guys as well as a fact sheet; other times, there were letters, personally signed by all five guys.

"We're sorry that it's taken a while for us to reply, we had no idea that so many of you would write to us—WOW, what a surprise!" read one fan club letter from 1990. "We lead pretty hectic lives and one problem with constantly touring is that we never stay in one place long enough to get close to folk. We've met some really nice girls on tour, but none of us has a steady date at the moment, that's why it's nice to know that we have special friends like you all over the world thinking about us. If it wasn't for good friends like you, the New Kids On The Block wouldn't be where we are now and we just want you to know just how much we appreciate your support."

The "we don't have girlfriends" refrain was a constant message in the early days. As part of the marketing strategy, the Kids had to be "everyone's boyfriend." When each of the guys' moms—Marlene Putnam, Alma Conroy (previously Wahlberg), Katherine McIntyre, and Betty Wood—appeared on *The Oprah Winfrey Show* in November 1990, Oprah pointed out that one of the biggest questions fans always had was, "Do the New Kids have girlfriends?" Betty replied, "They have lots and lots of girlfriends . . . they're enjoying themselves as young men of fame."

The moms, in fact, weren't just New Kids On The Block fan club organizers, they also became NKOTB ambassadors. In 1990, they, along with some of the Kids' fathers, did their own tour of various JCPenney locations around the country, to meet with fans and sign autographs; it was to promote the boys' first authorized biography, *Our Story.*

"It is difficult at times," Alma told *People.* "But the fans really are wonderful. They'll apologize for invading your privacy. . . . You can't help but get caught up in the excitement when a stadium full of kids are calling you by name!"

Jordan said his mom had other involvement, too. In a 1989 interview, he divulged that when fans threw their bras on stage, he kept them to give to her.

It was this wholesomeness that only helped grow the fanbase. "In a way, they were safe," author Rebecca Wallwork told *The Guardian* during an interview to promote her book, *Hangin' Tough.* "Parents allowed their kids to become quite obsessed with them because it wasn't a bad obsession." JCPenney's Business Planning Manager in the '90s, David Sube, corroborated that, telling *Daily Press*, "This is a good, clean group that the company likes."

Rebecca, who's an admitted Blockhead, also has another theory about why New Kids were so big in their heyday and continue to fuel nostalgic fans—when they got started, they played to a very important demographic that were in the prime of finding themselves. "Music cognition specialists said that what you listen to at 13 and 14 is what sticks with you and what you come back to," she told *The Guardian.* "Because that's a time when we're establishing our identity, and it's a time [when] your hormones are going crazy, so music has that same effect. And it's so powerful at that age that it imprints in such an impactful way."

There's also the ongoing interaction that members of NKOTB have with fans that continues to carry over. "That's the reason we're so big, because we try to be in contact with our fans," Joey told *Entertainment Tonight* in 1989. Even today, New Kids On The Block organizes fan cruises (an annual event first

Danny during a show in New York, circa 1990.

Fans greet their favorite band in September 1990.

established in 2009), as well as the first-ever fan convention in 2023—events at which the diehards can get up close and personal with each of the five guys. Fans can still sign up for the fan club today—now called Block Nation—with membership providing "first access" to buying tickets for shows and events as well as "exclusive gifts."

In 2017, NKOTB released the *Thankful* EP, and the title track was in large part inspired by the fans that have continued to stick by them all these years. "Each day, we are extremely thankful to have a unique relationship with all of you," New Kids On The Block wrote on Facebook in 2017, captioning a post celebrating the release of the "Thankful" music video. "You make us happy when we might be down, and make us feel connected when we might be alone. This video celebrates all of us."

A LIFE-CHANGING MEETING FOR TWO NKOTB FANS

Being a New Kids On The Block fan is more than just fun and games—it actually saved one woman's life. In August 2023, local news and *Good Morning America* picked up the story of a woman named Theresa Crockett (below), from Orange County, California, who received the life-changing gift of a kidney from a fellow New Kids On The Block fan. And it was all thanks to the intervention of Donnie Wahlberg.

Theresa has a chronic, hereditary condition called polycystic kidney disease that causes growths on her organs. Since 2020, she's been desperate to find a donor who would participate in a kidney transplant that could help extend her life. Unable to find one, and running out of time, Crockett had the idea to create a handmade sign about her search for a donor and brought it to a New Kids On The Block show she attended in May 2022. Theresa thought it could possibly help her find a match—and she was right.

Donnie spotted Theresa and her heart-shaped posterboard in the front of the crowd. "He folded it and said, 'I got you, I got you,' and when he said those words and gave us fist pumps, it's exactly what I needed to hear," Theresa told KABC-TV in Los Angeles. Donnie stepped up to the mic and shared Theresa's sign and her message with the thousands in attendance at the Honda Center in Anaheim, California. Theresa's son, Connor, filmed the whole thing and posted it to TikTok, where it went viral. A good number of NKOTB fans stepped up to get tested to see if they were a potential match, but none were.

Donnie kept Theresa's sign and brought it with him to the NKOTB fan cruise months later, where it caught the attention of Wisconsin-based physician Christina Meyer. She too wanted to be a donor, and after undergoing testing, was confirmed to be a match. At the end of August 2023, the kidney transplant happened, with Christina's organ flown from Wisconsin to California.

Donnie in particular has kept the story close to his heart, offering to bring both ladies on the NKOTB 2024 fan cruise, all expenses paid. "We're going to make shirts for the sailaway party," Theresa told *San Gabriel Valley Tribune*. "Mine's gonna say 'the new kidney on the block.'" She added that the members of the band have "hearts of gold" and have kept tabs on her progress throughout the ensuing months. "I know it sounds crazy, but this fandom is a family, and the army that I have behind me now with the situation proves it."

"What I'm doing now with producing is all stuff I've developed myself . . . it feels like I've earned it a lot more."

—Donnie on *The Joan Rivers Show* in 1992

Marky Mark and the Funky Bunch, circa 1990.

CHAPTER FIFTEEN

SPREADING THE GOOD VIBRATIONS

After helping to steer NKOTB's '91 effort, No More Games: The Remix Album, Donnie was hungry to do more production work. Especially as the New Kids were feeling a growing backlash to their own music.

"As New Kids got more successful—and got more criticism—that inspired me to write and produce music," Donnie shared with *Variety* in 2019. His first project: working with his younger brother, twenty-year-old Mark Wahlberg.

Mark had previously been in New Kids On The Block, albeit for a very short stint in 1984. He was recruited at the same time as Donnie, though the younger Wahlberg soon bailed on the project.

"He really wasn't into it. The first day we started going over to Maurice's house or the studio, I was into everything, I was playing the drums, I was trying to learn how to play everything and Mark was just like, 'I wanna

go with my friends and play basketball. This is not for me,'" Donnie told Arsenio Hall in a 1991 appearance on his talk show, adding, "Because it was all love songs and stuff like that and that's just not really what he wanted to do."

Ahead of Donnie helping his sibling put together his music project—Marky Mark and the Funky Bunch—Mark had also hit a personal rough patch. At fourteen, he dropped out of school, joined a gang, and struggled with drug addiction.

In 1986, he allegedly hurled rocks and screamed racial slurs at a group of Black elementary students. Two years later, in 1988, he was convicted of a racist hate crime after

Mark and Donnie in 1991.

he attacked two Vietnamese men. Upon arrest, he was charged with attempted murder, though it was later lessened to a criminal contempt charge. Mark was sentenced to two years in prison but only served 45 days in Deer Island House of Correction in Boston, the same institution the Wahlbergs' older brother served time at (and where NKOTB had one of their first concerts).

Mark eventually turned his life around with the help of Donnie, who knew his brother needed to find a passion project. "I told him if I ever got the chance I would help him do what he wanted to do," Donnie told Arsenio, and he did just that, helping Mark get a recording contract and producing ten of the eleven songs on Marky Mark and the Funky Bunch's debut album, 1991's *Music For The People*. (Danny Wood also produced one of the songs on the record.) In addition to Mark, the Funky Bunch included an all-Black ensemble featuring Scottie Gee, DJ-T, and Ashley Ace, meant to give the project a "street feel."

The first single was the wildly popular "Good Vibrations," featuring a sample of disco/R&B singer Loleatta Holloway's song "Love Sensation." It hit No. 1 on the *Billboard Hot 100* chart and stayed there for two weeks.

Its follow-up, "Wildside," also cracked the Top 10 and, together, the two tracks helped push *Music For The People* album sales past the 1 million mark. A second album, *You Gotta Believe*, came in 1992 but soon Mark left music behind to move into modeling (donning those famous tighty whities for Calvin Klein) and then, of course, acting.

Still, Donnie told *Variety*, everything all transpired the way it was supposed to. "Mark was meant to be on the path he's on. . . . I don't know if the success of the New Kids would have happened [if Mark stayed in the band]. I think Joey McIntyre filled the role that Mark would have filled, had Mark stayed. Mark's talent speaks for itself, but I'm not sure that Mark Wahlberg would've been a better Joey McIntyre than Joey McIntyre!"

Not only that, but working on *Music For The People* gave Donnie new purpose, as he also shared with *Variety*. "I wrote those songs to prove myself to the world as a songwriter and producer. It gave me a great chance to help Mark get off the streets and find something to do with his life, and also for me to have a voice outside of Maurice Starr."

Donnie's activity outside New Kids became so publicized that rumors started swirling that he was soon going to go solo. A few years later, he admitted to the *Baltimore Sun*, "In 1989, I initially had thoughts of leaving the group. I think that's when I sort of started probably rebelling a little bit, and branching off from the goody-goody thing." Rather than saying goodbye to the fame and fortune, however, he put his energy into developing his brother Mark. "When I produced my brother's first album, I could have easily done a lot of that stuff for myself," he added. "Those songs were songs that I just created with my musical taste."

MORE BOY BANDS TAKE OVER THE '90s

As Donnie was branching out with Marky Mark, the massive New Kids influence was finding its own extensions, with a new crop of boy bands coming to the surface. It was largely the work of now-disgraced scion Lou Pearlman, who was so impressed by the success (and money-making potential) of New Kids On The Block that he figured he'd try to become the next Maurice Starr.

The idea popped into Lou's head when he leased one of the planes from his aviation company fleet to NKOTB and was shocked to learn of the group's earnings. Lou brought on Johnny Wright (NKOTB's road manager) to help him. Soon he founded a record label, Trans Continental Records, and got to work discovering his boy band minions. He placed an ad in the *Orlando Sentinel* in 1993, and an open casting call soon netted the five talents who would become his first act, the Backstreet Boys (right). He followed that up with NSYNC, then O-Town, Take Five, and LFO. Lou was later sued by several of the acts and then sentenced to a twenty-five-year prison term, largely related to charges of fraud, conspiracy, and money laundering. He died in prison in 2016.

Yet, the New Kids never thought of the new crop as competition and have always cheered on boy band version 2.0 (in later years, they even toured and recorded with Backstreet Boys). As Donnie told CNN in 2009, "I found no bother in other boy bands taking the spotlight for a number of reasons: A, I was not interested in that spotlight myself. B, It was their time. C, We weren't even in a band anymore. I was doing other things." He added, "Anybody who was as successful as those guys were—be it Backstreet or NSYNC—it takes so much hard work to be successful. I can only respect [that]. We had a backlash on us, so to come out as a boy band after us and to have the perseverance to succeed and overcome a lot of doors that were closed from people hating on us . . . they deserve credit for that."

The band performs at the United Cerebral Palsy Telethon in 1991.

"Read my lips. These guys are not Milli Vanilli. The New Kids sing. They sang live on Arsenio three years ago and they'll do it again Wednesday."

—Maurice Starr talking to the *Los Angeles Times* in 1992

New Kids with Arsenio Hall, the day NKOTB received their star on the Hollywood Walk of Fame in 2014.

CHAPTER SIXTEEN

HEAR IT FROM THEIR LIPS

It was the bombshell heard around the world in late January 1992—were the New Kids On The Block actually lip-syncing the whole time? That was the allegation made by Gregory McPherson, a music teacher at the University of Massachusetts who was a short-lived music director for the group and helped produce some of their albums.

Gregory participated in an interview with the *New York Post* that month, claiming that the Kids "contributed no more than 20% of the singing on any of their albums." Instead, what he alleged was that Maurice and his brother Michael Johnson did the bulk of the vocal work. Gregory said this was the case in a 1990 Coca-Cola commercial for the Magic Summer Tour as well as the entirety of the tour itself, when they had an eight-track tape "to supplement their singing."

Furthermore, Gregory claimed that Maurice had a knack for flawlessly mimicking the singers on record. "He's like a musical ventriloquist. It's amazing to watch him do it. He's so

exceptionally talented he can sound like five different guys," the music teacher recounted to the *Los Angeles Times* in another 1992 interview. He added, "I'm not saying the Kids don't sing on the records, mind you. Maurice always had them lay down vocal tracks. But I personally saw him sing over them later and fix them up."

Gregory said that the lip-syncing revelations first came to him in 1989 when he was initially hired by Maurice to help piece together a live band to play with the Kids for their first *Arsenio Hall Show* appearance (a musical ensemble was a standing requirement for any artist to appear on the show).

ABOVE: Danny, Joey, Donnie, Jordan, and Jonathan during an interview in the late 1980s.

RIGHT: Arsenio Hall, circa 1990.

"Dick Scott (the group's co-manager with Maurice Starr) was walking around the studio shaking like a leaf on a tree. Everybody was so nervous about how rough the Kids sounded," Gregory shared in the interview. "[Dick] kept asking me how we could enhance their voices for the television appearance. I told him our only alternative was to buy this expensive synthesizer to digitally reproduce their voices and use it on the air. So they bought the synth immediately and had it flown in from California the next day."

The mechanism was supposed to recreate an exact copy of how the vocals sound on the record, which would then be mixed at a higher volume than the live vocals, but a malfunction happened during the live taping of *The Arsenio Hall Show*. The synth's vocals kept skipping and repeating, which made it seem that NKOTB were miming the lyrics and doing so out of order.

"It was embarrassing for everybody, to say the least," Gregory told the paper.

The allegations might never have blown up as much as they did had Gregory not filed a breach of contract lawsuit in Suffolk Superior Court in Boston on January 24, 1992, looking for compensation and restitution for his work on several hit-making NKOTB songs. When it seemed the suit wasn't going anywhere, he brought forth the lip-syncing allegations—and as soon as New Kids got word, they immediately pounced on the claims, ones that they said were another example of "jealous former business associates."

"I never once sang voice-overs on any New Kids' songs," Maurice told the *Los Angeles Times*. "These allegations are simply not true." And he had support. Richard Mendelson also spoke to the paper, backing up Maurice's assertions. Richard was the owner of Syncro Sound Studio in Boston and was an engineer on albums like *Step By Step*. "Maurice may be a marketing genius, but he is not singing on these songs. Whether you love them or hate them, that's the New Kids singing," said Richard.

The war of words continued. The *Los Angeles Times* also spoke to Florida-based composer James Cappra (who wrote NKOTB's 1986 song "Angel"), a former NKOTB tour production manager named John Wright, and Sugarhill Records rep Bernard Thomas (who was in the studio for *Step By Step* sessions), all of whom agreed with Gregory's claims. "Maurice Starr *is* the New Kids on the Block,"

Bernard told the paper. "The Kids do sing, but the voice you hear on the hits is Maurice. I've seen him sing over in the studio."

The sensitivity around the whole issue was really a matter of timing—not only were New Kids entering an impasse in their career in '92 as interest and sales began a downward tick, and they certainly did not need the bad publicity, but the lip-syncing allegations ran concurrent with claims that the European uber group Milli Vanilli was doing the same. Once proven, the dance duo had to give back their Grammys and pay back fans who bought albums and tickets.

So pivotal was it to refute the allegations that New Kids On The Block halted the Australian leg of their No More Games Tour in February 1992 to return to *The Arsenio Hall Show* to prove they were singing live. Fans were in the audience who backed up their favorite band— "I've seen them in concert eight times over the last year and I don't think it's true," said one, providing her own kind of evidence: "You can hear occasional bad notes."

Maurice, of course, joined the group and participated in a brief Q&A with Arsenio before the performance, in which he adamantly asserted, "All their leads [vocals] have always been live." When asked if he had sung on any of the New Kids albums, Maurice responded, "Only background with the guys. I'm pretty sure anyone in here would've loved to have sung backgrounds with New Kids on the albums." Cheers erupted from the crowd.

With Maurice firmly planted in his seat in the audience, the five New Kids took to the stage to deliver a two-song set. At one point, Donnie took lead on a song break and said, "I've got something to say about all this nonsense going on," before devolving into a

A WHOLE LOTTA LIP SERVICE

New Kids On The Block were hardly the first act to be accused of lip-syncing. In addition to Milli Vanilli, Britney Spears, Mariah Carey, and even Whitney Houston, many singers have allegedly used some backing support. Still, the fallout was inescapable for NKOTB after Gregory's allegations came to light.

In Chicago, a fan filed a $75 million class-action lawsuit claiming the New Kids "defrauded everyone who bought their music." In February 1992, NKOTB also filed their own defamation suit against Gregory, who (like James Cappra) eventually retracted the lip-syncing allegations and dropped his lawsuit in April of that year. It's reported Gregory reached a six-figure settlement with Maurice, including promises to appear on upcoming projects helmed by the star-maker. However, Gregory told the *Los Angeles Times* that his and Maurice's pastors were a large part of the amends: "We were setting a poor example as Christians for kids in the community."

The New Kids claim they were not only hurt by Gregory's allegations, but even more so by how many media outlets ran with the story without their perspective—and in so doing, they believed tarnished the reputation of the band. "What really made us mad was that, when the truth finally came out, it barely got reported," Jordan told the *LA Times*. "Everybody jumped on the bandwagon with all the negative stuff about how we didn't sing, but . . . nobody did any stories saying the guy who spread all these lies admitted he was a fraud. Nobody printed any big headlines like, 'The New Kids Really Do Sing!' . . . It's like everybody in the world thinks you're a big phony. Even though you know you didn't do what you're being accused of, you have to live with the fact that people want to believe the worst."

volatile rap that he said he wrote on the plane on the way back to the US. He hurled insults Gregory's way, referring to him as a "bitch" and a "sucker."

In the post-performance interview, the New Kids noted that Gregory McPherson was let go from the group and said they believed that the lawsuit and allegations were part of a scheme to pilfer money from them at the peak of their success; the band said Gregory was never in the studio any time they cut vocal tracks and wouldn't even have knowledge of the inner workings.

"We never claimed to be great singers . . . if you've read any record review from the last three years, it says, 'New Kids can't sing,' 'they sing lousy on the record.' . . . It makes it all the more ridiculous why everyone all of a sudden believes that a really, really great singer who's been singing for over 20 years, Maurice Starr, could be the voice on those records," Donnie told long-time ally Arsenio. Throughout the band's career, Arsenio has remained a staunch supporter of the group. In the early years, he was one of the first to provide a late-night stage for the band in 1989 to perform their burgeoning hits and then allowed the Kids the space to refute those lip-synching claims in 1992. By 2014, Arsenio helped fete NKOTB when they received their star on the Hollywood Walk of Fame, giving a heartfelt induction speech. A year prior, in 2013, during a short-lived reboot of *The Arsenio Hall Show*, the host invited Donnie back to promote *Blue Bloods*, with Arsenio referring to the actor/singer as "my dog." When Donnie sat down for the one-on-one chat, he responded to the screaming fan reaction, saying, "I think they're cheering because they know how much I respect you. . . . This audience, they grew up with me and they know how much of a part you played in my career."

New Kids perform in London in October 1991.

"If you think New Kids is gonna be dead in two months and you're right, good for you. . . . Every music group is gonna fade out sooner or later. If we never make another record in our lives, who cares?"

—Donnie talking to the *Phoenix New Times* in 1994

NKOTB climb the ladder of success in the late 1980s.

CHAPTER SEVENTEEN

NEW KIDS FACE THE MUSIC

The lip-synching allegations (even though they were eventually retracted) were the final domino piece that made the whole New Kids empire really start to crumble. Two short years later, in 1994, the group would ultimately announce a breakup, after attempts to regroup and rebrand.

But even in 1992, there were signs that interest in the band was waning. The $74 million in record-breaking concert ticket sales that made NKOTB the top-grossing concert act of 1990 were all but forgotten in 1991; the rebranded No More Games Tour didn't even crack the Top 10 list put out by *Pollstar* that year.

Granted, the industry magazine claimed it was a "bad year" in general for concert ticket sales and New Kids spent most of the 1991–'92 leg of the tour overseas, but they still had a significant 42 dates in the US that failed to

track. The top-grossing acts of '91 included the Grateful Dead, ZZ Top, the Judds, Rod Stewart, Paul Simon, Guns N' Roses, Bell Biv DeVoe, Michael Bolton, Garth Brooks, and Clint Black.

Discerning music tastes within the pivotal teen demographic were becoming a hindrance—poppy boy bands were out and grunge rock and rap were largely in. A story in the *Press Telegram* declared "grunge [and] rap music movements of the early 1990s became Gen X's soundtrack," citing artists such as Nirvana, Dr. Dre, Pearl Jam, and 2Pac as

Nirvana in the early 1990s.

essential listening in the early '90s. Both genres gave voice to millions of disenfranchised young people who were done sugarcoating things.

"Grunge came along, and in some ways, that was a reason we went away," Joey declared to *ET Canada* in 2022. Though, he also conceded, "We needed time to grow as people, we were nonstop for five years there."

The band actually did take a short break in that crucial time period between 1992 and 1994, largely abstaining from releasing new music (besides a late single in December 1993) and taking the time to rebrand. In this period,

they also split ways with Maurice Starr, who the *Boston Herald* claims left the city in 1993, relocating to his native Florida to try it again with a new crop of boy bands like NK5 and the HeartBeat Boys. None of his future protégés would ever reach the level of New Kids On The Block, however.

Even so, the New Kids have always seemed to keep Maurice close to heart, reuniting with him at a few pivotal moments over the years, including their Hollywood Walk of Fame induction in 2014 and when Maurice came to a stop on NKOTB's Mixtape Tour in 2022. Their former producer/manager suffered a stroke in 2015 that has since debilitated him, making his reunion with the Kids even more meaningful. According to Maurice's nephew Bobby, the music mogul was "determined to meet up and reunite with five guys from Boston, whom he loves tremendously."

Back in 1992, however, as New Kids On The Block attempted to distance themselves from Maurice after the lip-syncing scandal, they also tried to makeover their image. Having shortened their name to NKOTB initially on the *No More Games: The Remix Album* in late 1990, the five-piece stuck with the acronym to appear more mature and move farther away from the Kids image (to drive that point home, many members now sported facial hair, too). It was a natural pivot as the members moved squarely into their twenties. "We're not New anymore and we're not Kids anymore," Jordan said in an appearance on *Live with Regis and Kathie Lee*.

In 1993, the members regrouped in the studio and began work on their fifth LP, *Face The Music*. Released in 1994, it came four years after *Step By Step*, a solid year-and-a-half after taking a break from the spotlight, and was a total about-face from all their previous releases.

Phoenix New Times shared some of the revamped NKOTB bio distributed to media by Columbia Records in 1994, which read in part that the band members "have matured . . . with a razor-sharp musical direction—and a street-savvy edge to their still irresistible sound," while also hailing "NKOTB is into [sic] fearlessly plunging into the cutting edge of the hip-hop Nineties."

Most notably, Maurice Starr's name is nowhere on *Face The Music*. Donnie did a

good chunk of the writing and production—on the album, he's credited for the first time as an arranger, composer, executive producer, multi-instrumentalist, and producer, and is also noted for his rapping and vocal contributions. Danny is credited as an arranger, composer, multi-instrumentalist, producer, and for his contributions with mixing and vocals. Joey likewise appears in the liner notes for composing, programming, and vocals. Jordan is credited as an executive producer and for his

Jordan attends the 1999 MTV Video Music Awards in New York.

Joey, Jordan, Donnie, Danny, and Jonathan attend the 1994 American Music Awards in Los Angeles.

programming and vocal work. The only name notably missing is Jonathan, who typically let the other band members drive the efforts on all the band's albums. NKOTB were also joined in the studio by luminaries including new jack swing kingpin Teddy Riley, the Sylvers' Leon Sylvers III, Walter Afanasieff (a then go-to for Mariah Carey and Celine Dion), and hip-hop duo Nice & Smooth, among others.

Speaking to MTV ahead of the album drop, Donnie said *Face The Music* wasn't as much a comeback for the band as it was a "new beginning," and that the band wasn't concerned with having the same returns as they did in the late '80s/early '90s. They were just

content with the music they were producing on their own terms.

The first single was the R&B-soul fusion track "If You Go Away," which was originally released in late 1991 as a standalone that appeared on the *H.I.T.S.* album, the band's first "greatest hits" record issued by Columbia, and was then repurposed for *Face The Music*. It was also one of the tracks NKOTB performed on *The Arsenio Hall Show* to rebuke the lip-synching claims. The song is also notable for being the last NKOTB track to date to place in the Top 20 of the *Billboard Hot 100* chart.

"Dirty Dawg" was the next pre-release single, released in December 1993 and including rap verses from Nice & Smooth. The final single from *Face The Music* was "Never Let You Go," also the final single NKOTB would release before reuniting in 2008. Another standout track on the album is "Keep on Smilin," which was on the *Free Willy* music soundtrack in 1993.

Face The Music received some high marks from critics, though other reviews were still less favorable. *AllMusic* said, "The New Kids return after much ridicule and doubt with the defensive *Face the Music*, and, surprise!—it isn't bad at all. Sure, they've changed their style a bit—their new jack R&B is a bit rougher, the lyrics are a touch nastier, and their hip-hop sounds a little more real—but none of it sounds fake, and the best tracks on the album might impress even the most jaded listener."

But, in a pitiful star-and-a-half review in the *Los Angeles Times*, the reviewer chided the album with, "They can run, but they can't hide: It'll take more than an acronym trick for those New Kids On The Block to pull the wool over our eyes. *Face the Music* represents the vocal quintet's bid at holding onto its old bubblegum audience while moving boldly ahead toward earning its hip-hop 'props.' The first few cuts, designed to establish NKOTB's newfound street savvy, are particularly embarrassing."

Phoenix New Times also declared, "Any advances in NKOTB's mastery of R&B are strictly infinitesimal. The songs, filled with NutraSweet balladeering and diluted hip-hop, will make you forget neither the savvy harmonies of Boyz II Men nor the mad science of Prince."

Sales for *Face The Music* were a far cry from NKOTB's heyday just a few years prior. Only 138,000 total units were sold, and the album placed at No. 37 on the *Billboard 200*

chart. In an interview with *Phoenix New Times*, Donnie put a large part of the blame on what was called "low-key" promotion by Columbia Records and perhaps also the backlash that came from trying to suddenly flip the switch on how NKOTB was marketed.

"What we always talk about with them [Columbia] is we've been overmarketed. I think we've been represented by images that were a lot of times never approved by us," he shared with the paper, adding, "People saw the marketing potential and wanted to capitalize on it. There was no time or desire to oversee how we were being marketed."

The poor album traction carried over into the band's tour to promote it. Gone were the sold-out crowds at venues like Dodger Stadium; NKOTB was relegated to small clubs and theaters for a short month-long run in the spring of 1994.

The *New York Times* reviewed one of the very first dates at the now shuttered Academy Theatre in the Big Apple on April 2, noting, "The set on Saturday night was low key compared with the shows the group used to present at sold-out arenas. Featuring a six-man, all-Black band and three dancers, N.K.O.T.B. mixed urban American slang, Black choreography, and the contemporary, hip-hop-influenced rhythm-and-blues style known as new jack swing. But even with all these signifiers of hipness and its very authentic wardrobe, the group seemed contrived, and the set was mostly as corny as an old Osmond Brothers clip." Though the reviewer did have one high point, noting that Donnie's "forays into rapping were less awkward than they used to be."

The tour wasn't short of drama either. Early on, Jonathan decided to sit it out. Initially it

JUST SAY NO TO REUNIONS

There were several attempts made by outside sources to reunite New Kids On The Block, though all of them failed. First came an offer from MTV to have the Fab Five reunite for a performance at the 1999 VMAs, just as boy bandemonium was taking over the channel. Joey told the *Boston Globe* it was a no-go when Jonathan decided he wasn't ready to take the stage again. That didn't stop Jordan from appearing on the broadcast, however; he was up for his own VMA award for "Best Dance Video" for his solo track "Give It To You" (he lost to Ricky Martin's "Livin' la Vida Loca").

Another NKOTB reunion offer came in 2004, this time for VH1's short-lived ambush program *Bands Reunited,* which attempted to bring defunct acts back together through guerilla tactics. Host Aamer Haleem all but stalked out the individual members of NKOTB on the streets of Boston, Miami (where Danny relocated), and New York City (where Joey was starring on Broadway), even going so far as to set up mock interviews while trying to get them all to agree to do a one-night-only comeback show.

"I don't think you can get us together," Jordan defiantly told Aamer. Surprisingly, Jonathan signed on for the opportunity, as did Jordan (each signed a record that acted like a quasi-contract). Yet Joey was the holdout this time, telling the host, "I wouldn't want to do it this way, if we all got together, I'd want it to be because it had a long-term plan. . . . Something we were all on the same page for." Danny and Donnie also refused the offer and didn't appear on camera, noting they were either out of the biz or focusing on acting, respectively.

All five members had been adamant over the years that they wouldn't reunite unless everyone was on board with the idea. That, of course, finally happened in 2008 (below).

The New Kids, photographed in 1994.

was blamed on a back injury he allegedly sustained while riding a horse; years later, it would be revealed that Jonathan was suffering from crippling anxiety and panic attacks, and the stress of performances and touring had become too much for him by '94. Even during TV appearances to promote the new album, Jonathan was notably absent. During a taping of British show *Live & Kicking*, he was said to be sick. As he told Oprah Winfrey in a 2001 appearance on her talk show to discuss panic disorder, "The whole New Kids thing was crazy. . . . The more it grew, the more I just felt like I was trapped. I just always had this feeling inside me of always being nervous and afraid of situations."

Without their fifth bandmate and seeing the downshift in fan reception, NKOTB canceled remaining dates and officially pulled the plug on the band as well by June of that year.

Anyone who had watched broadcast appearances or read interviews could see it coming. The band seemed exhausted, burnt out, absent, and just not into it anymore. On *Live with Regis and Kathie Lee,* Donnie even made jabs at his bandmates, noting how he never got any time away from them. Jordan fought with British journalists (notably Piers Morgan) during a UK PR blitz when asked about Brit boy band Take That. Several archived pieces of interview footage from '94 on YouTube are labeled as "awkward" or "sleepy."

Some might have said the band quit at the right time, and the decision likely paved the way for a lucrative reunion fourteen years later— though the band members didn't go silently into the night. Even riding solo, they were still a big part of the pop culture consciousness heading into the 2000s.

THE '00s

HANGIN' TOUGH

The New Kids attend the 2008
MuchMusic Video Awards.

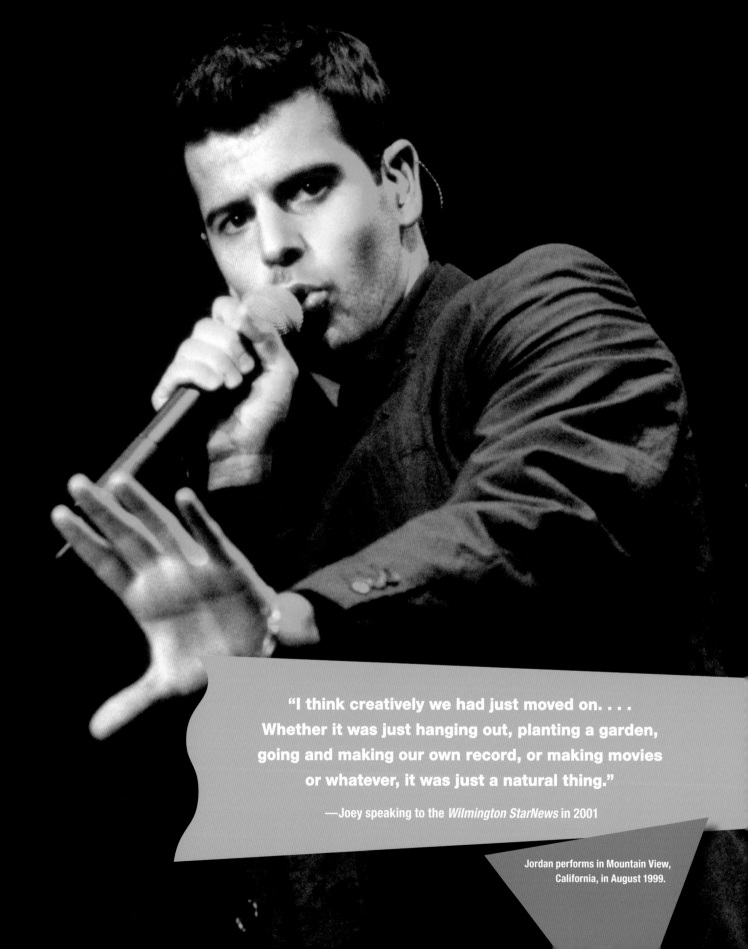

"I think creatively we had just moved on. . . .
Whether it was just hanging out, planting a garden,
going and making our own record, or making movies
or whatever, it was just a natural thing."

—Joey speaking to the *Wilmington StarNews* in 2001

Jordan performs in Mountain View,
California, in August 1999.

CHAPTER EIGHTEEN

GOING SOLO

Even before NKOTB officially broke up in June 1994, rumors had started circulating that the band was near its end and that members were eyeing solo careers. In a 1990 story, *Washington Post* hinted at the idea, noting how several members had already begun to collaborate outside the circle: Jordan with an emerging teeny bopper named Anna, Donnie with a Japanese singing star named Seiko, and Joey apparently trying to get a duet going with none other than classic crooner Frank Sinatra.

On *The Arsenio Hall Show* in 1992, Donnie explained a solo album *could* come, but that he wasn't the only one in the boy band looking to spread their wings. "I may do a solo album but Jordan is also maybe doing a solo album. Danny is producing two albums," Donnie told Arsenio, adding, "We're all just getting away from it, we all want to let all the hype die down, let everyone just take a break, clear our heads, and come back together in a year or so and kick ass another time."

Of course, that break would ultimately be a lot more definitive, and it would be fourteen years before they came back together again.

In an interview with *Wilmington StarNews* in 2001, Joey confirmed that NKOTB parted ways because each member was wanting to "try different things." The idea of splitting up actually came around the time *Step By Step* was completed, when they were all "on their own separate islands."

The first tastes of what they could do on their own came in 1999, when both Joey and Jordan released their solo debuts. Joey's album, *Stay The Same*, was a return to his humble roots—not only the theatrical pop he got his feet wet with, but also in how the album was approached. He used his own money to fund the recording and, rather than tap into a major distributor like NKOTB had, he sold the thirteen-track effort on his website. Joey also circulated copies to local radio DJs in Boston.

According to an interview with *Entertainment Tonight* around the time of the album's release, Joey did try shopping the album around but, surprisingly, couldn't find any labels that would give him a record deal. "We didn't sit around saying, you know, somebody sign me and make me a star. We said, let's go get 'em," he told the outlet. Before long, the album took off and Columbia Records (NKOTB's original label) eventually signed Joey as a solo artist. They released *Stay The Same* under the label subsidiary C2 Records.

Stay The Same's title track ("about believing in yourself and doing your best to use the individual gifts you have") was a verified hit, reaching No. 10 on the *Billboard Hot 100* chart, and the album itself was eventually gold certified. Notably, several of Joey's New Kids cohorts were included in the liner notes: Donnie is credited on the songs "Give It Up," "Because Of You," and "We Can Get Down," while Danny is credited on "Let Me Take You For A Ride" and "One Night." Even with the split, the five Kids appeared to remain amicable. As Joey told *Entertainment Tonight*, "That's all you can ask for, to still come out friends."

To promote the album, Joey joined another burgeoning pop star on stage, filming "Britney Spears And Joey McIntyre In Concert" at Disneyland. It was for a TV special that aired on the Disney Channel in 1999, just as Britney was deep into her *. . . Baby One More Time* tour debut.

In 1999, Jordan also released his eponymous solo debut, a searing soul and dance pop effort that launched with the sexy club single "Give It To You" in February. The song landed in the No. 10 spot on the *Billboard Hot 100* chart; a second single, a cover of Prince's "I Could Never Take The Place Of Your Man," came in July of that year. Curiously, much of the album featured writing contributions from Robin Thicke, who was unknown at the time; it was a solid fourteen years before Robin's song "Blurred Lines" would propel him into the mainstream. Like Joey's debut, Jordan's first solo record also featured the handiwork of his New Kids colleagues, with Donnie credited on the song, "Don't Run." Elsewhere on Jordan's album, production work comes from noted R&B/pop production team Jimmy Jam and Terry Lewis.

Jordan did have a record deal for his solo album. He'd signed to Interscope Records initially in 1996, though it took him almost four years and a number of producers to home in on his sound as a solo artist. But the timing couldn't have been more perfect for Jordan and Joey to make their one-man debuts, as pop music was taking over as the cultural touchpoint in 1999, with Britney Spears and a new wave of boy bands like Backstreet Boys, NYSNC, and 98 Degrees dominating the charts. "The music landscape changing to more pop music definitely is helping me out like crazy," Jordan told the *Los Angeles Times* at the time.

Interscope also used their marketing muscle to help push the material out to MTV, VH1, and BET, among others. "Give It To You" was a big radio hit for Jordan, and he was even nominated for an MTV VMA in 1999 for one of the music videos. *Jordan Knight* peaked at No. 29 on the *Billboard 200* chart and sold 500,000-plus copies in the US. Jordan also did a brief tour with 98 Degrees that summer to help promote it.

Jordan and Joey's solo careers would continue to remain active in the 2000s. As Jordan told journalist Heather Byrd in 2010, "I don't want to do songs like I'm 18 years old. I want to do cool, hip records but also they have to have a maturity about them. They have to reflect me and where I'm at. . . . What's inspiring me now are life experiences. I think what's different now for me is I'm a little more grown into me, I feel more comfortable in my own skin. I feel more comfortable on stage. Twenty years ago, going on stage, I was kind of shell-shocked and now it's like I feel a little more relaxed. I soak it up more. I don't take it for granted."

Throughout the early 2000s, Joey would release his sophomore solo work, *Meet Joe Mac* (2001), which produced the hit song "Rain." There was also a live album called *One Too Many: Live from New York* (2002), recorded at a show at Joe's Pub in New York, in which Joey teamed up with guitarist Emanuel Kiriakou for a series of his originals, NKOTB songs, and covers like Fleetwood Mac's "Landslide" and U2's "One." There was one more original work in the '00s, the album *8:09* (2004), while 2006's *Talk To Me* was a crooners covers album, featuring Joey's takes on "Moon River" and "The Way You Look Tonight," among others.

Jordan had a few more solo works to offer in the 2000s, as well, including *Jordan Knight Performs New Kids On The Block: The Remix Album* (2004), in which he re-recorded NKOTB's biggest hits under his solo banner; 2005's *The Fix*; and *Love Songs* (2006), which was notably released on Trans Continental Records, the label owned by now-disgraced boy band mogul Lou Pearlman.

Danny also attempted to branch out as a solo artist in this decade, albeit at the more

mature age of 34. His first album, *Second Face,* came out in 2003 via BMG and failed to track like Joey's and Jordan's solo debuts had, perhaps a victim of poor timing. As *PopMatters* wrote in their review, "Danny Wood and *Second Face* will be the dying epitaph that should have been issued four years ago when it might have stood a chance. Now, it's just crumbs in the wind."

Joey at the Greek Theatre in Los Angeles in 1999.

THIS NEW KID GOES TO THE MARKET

Jonathan was first to leave New Kids On The Block in 1994, after years of debilitating panic attacks and anxiety. He felt the band had done their thing "long enough," as he told *People*, adding, "those attacks had a big impact on my determining to leave the entertainment industry."

So, Jonathan went home—and he basically never left. Jonathan's New Kids earnings had been enough for him to buy a sprawling twenty-acre estate in Essex, Massachusetts, where he lived in a farmhouse and had a horse stable. Although it sounds serene, it was a huge sea change and an incredibly unnerving time.

"It was probably the scariest time in my life," Jonathan told the *New York Times* in 2021. "I just remember being home for a few days, opening the door to my bedroom in the morning and looking around, and nobody's there. The New Kids weren't there. There were no tour buses. Everything was just done." He remembers falling into a state of depression until he got a call one day from a friend, a former Boston cop who had done some security work for the New Kids; he was looking for a partner to help him flip and sell houses. Jonathan immediately said yes and found his new passion. The singer estimates he's flipped about 200 estates since, focusing on historic farmhouses that are 100 years old or more.

"Restoring the American farmhouse is not just a hobby for me—it's my passion, my obsession," Jonathan told *People*. "I give it that love, show it that respect and bring it back to its glory."

It became such a lucrative project that HGTV even took note and approached Jonathan about starring in his own home renovation reality show. Since 2021, Jonathan has been hosting *Farmhouse Fixer* (left, with other HGTV stars) for the channel, in which he works with guest clients to restore their homes.

As he told *People*, the ultimate reward is "that moment they actually step in the door, it's so exciting and so relieving at the same time. You finally can breathe and say, 'We did it.'"

But much had happened for Danny in those interim years. At first, Danny tapped into the production instincts that he had developed during the New Kids years. In addition to being behind the boards on Joey's solo albums and working with pop group LFO, Danny was also behind the scenes on some TV and film productions. Life also took some turns as Danny engaged in a custody battle for his eldest son and helped his beloved mother, Betty, during her cancer battle. Sadly, Betty passed in 1999, and Danny put music to the side as he came to grips with her loss.

Many of his life experiences made it onto *Second Face*. Like Joey in the beginning, Danny too had a hard time trying to find a label to get behind the effort. "Most labels didn't like his association with the bygone pop group [NKOTB]," said *Tampa Bay Times* in their 2003 profile of the artist. Instead, Danny put his own money into producing the album before BMG came along. The first single, "When The Lights Go Out," was a radio hit in Florida. As Danny told the *Tampa Bay Times* about *Second Face*, "When you hear my record, nothing's going to remind you of a New Kids song. It's a mature record. I just wanted to make a record that I would listen to."

Following *Second Face*, Danny also put out two more albums in the 2000s: *Coming Home* (2008) and *Stronger: Remember Betty* (2009), the latter dedicated to his late mother. Proceeds were donated to the Susan G. Komen for the Cure foundation.

There were two New Kids On The Block members who totally abandoned music in the 2000s. Donnie, of course, made a different kind of debut: acting. Following in the footsteps of his brother Mark, Donnie's first roles were in films like the Mel Gibson-led *Ransom* (1996),

Danny photographed in Florida in May 2003.

Black Circle Boys (1997), *Southie* (1998), and *The Sixth Sense* (1999), the last one featuring Donnie in the gripping role of a disturbed young man, Vincent Gray, which all but put Donnie on the map in Hollywood. In 2009, he did end up releasing one music single with former Danity Kane member Aubrey O'Day, named "I Got It," that sparked rumors they were dating.

And Jonathan—well, he got out of entertainment altogether, went to live on a farm, and eventually started dabbling in real estate.

Joey joins Britney Spears and
Mickey Mouse in Disney World in 1999.

"I've never lived with a girl. I'm not at an age where I want to have a real girlfriend. One person for the rest of my life? That's ridiculous."

—Joey talking to *People* in 1990

Joey with then-fiancée, now-wife Barrett Williams in 2003.

CHAPTER NINETEEN

NEW KIDS BECOME FAMILY MEN

All the Kids spent years denying they had girlfriends, to keep their largely female fan base happy. As Donnie put it to *People*, "I got more girls liking me than I ever had in my life. When you have a few million girls who really like you, you don't want to disappoint them."

If anything came from the breakup of NKOTB, at least it allowed the guys to find true romance.

Danny was the first to get married and also the first to have a child. After a short-lived fling with actress Halle Berry in 1989 (apparently that one snuck past NKOTB fans), Danny started dating Elise Stepherson; together, they had a son, Daniel Jr., in 1993.

By 1997, he was married to a Miami songwriter by the name of Patricia Alfaro and they welcomed two daughters, Chance (who was adopted in Russia) and Vega. Upon marrying Patty, Danny relocated to Florida. The couple parted ways and finalized their divorce in 2006. Danny told *Entertainment Tonight* that the passing of his mother, Betty, put a strain on his relationship with his ex-wife.

"It had a big impact on my life because I didn't accept [my mother's death] for a long time," Danny shared. "She was so influential in my life that I just didn't accept it. Between me and my ex-wife, it was that for me and other issues for her, ending our marriage."

Though Danny has not remarried in the years since, he's celebrated being a grandpa

THE SINGLE YEARS

The New Kids On The Block sang countless songs about love and yearning at their shows night after night in the early '90s. They serenaded the largely female crowds with passionate pleas like "Please Don't Go Girl" and convincing testaments like "I'll Be Loving You (Forever)," which only made the fangirls fall even farther head over heels for their diehard crushes.

But, even with all the love they had to give, the New Kids stayed largely single during this time period—or at least kept relationships under the radar. Going public with any girlfriend during their heyday would have crushed the spirit of their undying fanbase and ruined the illusion that the guys were "everyone's boyfriends." *Full House* stars Candace Cameron-Bure and Andrea Barber were questioned by *TMZ* why they never dated a New Kid to which Barber responded, "they were too big." She even admitted that the *Full House* crew couldn't get the rights to have the band appear on the show or even have a poster on DJ Tanner's wall, let alone set up any kind of date.

But that didn't mean the guys didn't date in secret. In talking with *Boston Magazine* in 2021, Joey was asked, when they were all young and single, "who was the biggest player in the group?" To which he replied, "Well, the Three Amigos were Jordan [Knight], Donnie [Wahlberg], and Danny [Wood], you know? I don't know if anyone had more conquests than the other, but it was definitely like the Serengeti out there." Danny reportedly had a short relationship with Halle Berry (right) for a time in 1989, while Joey was linked to MTV VJ SuChin Pak before he wed his now-wife Barrett Williams in 2003. The one relationship that did go public in the '90s was between Jonathan and singer Tiffany who were tour mates at the time. But, knowing that Jonathan would come out as gay years later, that match may have been yet another strategy by the NKOTB team to diffuse any rumors.

after the birth of Rose Elizabeth Wood in 2019. The tot has been seen on her grandpa's YouTube lifestyle and cooking series, *The Wood Works*.

In 2019, Danny told *People*, "My kids are my biggest fans now. My daughters love coming to the shows and going on tour with me." He also laughed off his daughter Chance gushing over his fellow bandmates in an episode of New Kids On The Block's Pop TV reality series, *Rock This Boat*. "I guess it's part of the risk, you know, your daughters having a crush on one of the guys in the group," Danny said in the clip. "That has not been really enjoyable for me."

Donnie was the next one to say his vows. He met his soon-to-be first wife, a California-based recording engineer named Kim Fey, during sessions for the Marky Mark and the Funky Bunch albums. The two married in 1999 and had two sons, Xavier and Elijah, before divorcing in 2008. In fact, it was their split that reportedly was a catalyst for NKOTB to reunite. According to *Entertainment Tonight*, the divorce left Donnie heartbroken and depressed, and he sought new opportunities that could take his focus.

Eventually, Donnie would remarry in 2014, wedding actress and TV host Jenny McCarthy in a hotel in Illinois, where the couple now resides (all four of his bandmates were present for the nuptials). The couple first met when they appeared together on Bravo's *Watch What Happens Live* in 2012; a year later, Donnie made an appearance on her VH1 series, *The Jenny McCarthy Show*, in which they turned up the heat for the cameras, and they began a courtship that went official in July 2013.

In 2015, Donnie told *CBS This Morning*, "You know, her and I came through in the same era and have both gone through divorces and have gone through so many similarities, both professionally and personally, and to discover each other for the first time in our forties—we never really met through all those years—we just hit it off. We have very similar sort of mentalities and spiritualities and similar philosophies, we have so much in common. It's a really wonderful fit and I think we really complement each other."

The couple has also found opportunities to work together over the years: They co-starred in the short-lived reality series *Donnie Loves Jenny*; joined up as co-producers on Joey's TV series, *Return of The Mac*; and in 2021, Donnie was one of the mystery guests on competition show *The Masked Singer*, on which Jenny is a judge. Of course, Donnie and his bandmates were also guests on Jenny's former SiriusXM show.

In early 2023, Donnie helped his twenty-year-old stepson, Evan Asher (Jenny's son with ex John Asher), release his first-ever music single and video, for a song called "It Doesn't Matter," written in homage to Evan's Hollywood crush, Selena Gomez. Donnie enlisted his son Elijah to kick in some production work (Elijah is also a musician, recording under the nom de plume Pink Laces; his brother Xavier has also dabbled in some metal bands).

Jordan has had the longest relationship. He met his now-wife Evelyn Melendez in the latter part of the '90s. They had their first son Dante in 1999; a second son, Eric, followed in 2007.

On an appearance on *The Queen Latifah Show* in 1999, Jordan recounted the "miracle" it was to become a father for the first time, sharing, "I used to be like, 'I ain't changing nobody's diapers,' but when you see your cute little kid like that, you'd do anything for him."

Jordan also revealed to *Entertainment Tonight* that he serenaded his wife with an impromptu rendition of NKOTB's "I'll Be Loving You (Forever)" on their wedding day in 2004.

"There was a piano on wheels and a friend of mine pushed it in and was like, 'And now Jordan's going to sing, "I'll Be Loving You (Forever)!"'" He put me on the spot, so I sang it," Jordan recalled. "She loved it. When I was singing, I was really feeling it and meaning it, so I think she knew that. We both cried and it was definitely a beautiful moment." The song has long been a wedding staple for many New Kids devotees on their own big days.

Nowadays, Jordan and Evelyn are behind an Italian restaurant, Novara, in Milton, Massachusetts, where they reside. When it comes to the secret to his longstanding relationship, Jordan told *Entertainment Tonight*, "You have to tell your wife when you're going on tour. Let her know your plans. Don't tell her the day before or the week before—keep her in the loop!"

Joey and his wife Barrett Williams recently celebrated twenty years of marriage; they tied the knot in 2003, having met the year before when Barrett was a real estate agent showing Joey a potential house to buy in Los Angeles.

Donnie with wife Jenny McCarthy in 2014.

REMEMBERING BETTY WOOD

All the New Kids' moms (below is a photo of the band with their parents) hold a special place in the history of the band. When Danny's mom Betty Wood died in 1999 at the young age of fifty-five after a battle with breast cancer, Danny made sure her memory would live on by establishing the Remember Betty Foundation in 2015.

It came years after Danny and NKOTB fans had fundraised on behalf of larger cancer charities in honor of Betty. When NKOTB embarked on their reunion in 2008, the renewed fanbase gave Danny an even larger audience to spread the word. In fact, many merch items for the NKOTB reunion tour were decorated with pink ribbons with proceeds donated back to the 501(c)3 organization. All proceeds from Danny's 2009 album *Stronger: Remember Betty* went toward fundraising for a cure and, in 2014, Danny also ran the Boston Marathon to raise funds for Remember Betty. Joey McIntyre did the same in support of the Alzheimer's Association (the disease his mother died from that year).

The mission of the Remember Betty Foundation is to "help minimize the financial burden associated with breast cancer for patients and survivors so that they can focus on recovery and quality of life." Whether it's medical bills, rent, or something like car repairs, the foundation provides financial support so those stricken with the illness can more easily continue with treatment appointments.

Danny told *Entertainment Tonight* in 2018 that it touched his heart to see so many NKOTB fans jump in to help fundraise for the mission, even setting up their own local chapters in many cases.

"They started making Team Bettys all over the country and a lot of it comes from the fact that they've lost someone too," he shared. "Everyone's connected to breast cancer, specifically in our fan base. And the guys in the group are connected to it because they were all close with my mom. It's taken off to the point now where I've become friends with a lot of these girls who are fundraising. They still come to shows and fangirl, but some of them have my phone number and we talk about ideas they have for fundraisers. They're passionate about it because they're all connected to it, and some are survivors themselves."

Today, Remember Betty is featured prominently on the official NKOTB website where fans are linked directly to the organization's site to get more info and donate.

Jordan at his restaurant, Novara, in 2016.

Two decades and three kids later—their brood includes sons Griffin and Rhys, born in 2007 and 2009, respectively, and daughter Kira, born in 2011—and the family unit is still going strong, splitting their time between the coasts.

All the McIntyres appeared on Joey's scripted comedy show, *Return Of The Mac*, which debuted on Pop TV in 2017. He told the *New York Post* of working with his wife and kids, "My daughter seems like a natural in that she's got a dry sense of humor. My youngest son, Rhys, was a director's dream because he would hit his mark every time, it was amazing. And then my oldest son, he's a little bit more of a showman. Everybody had their [screen time], but my wife of course was like, 'It better be even.'"

These days, Joey's sons seem to be taking after him. Griffin appeared in a Netflix show called *Country Comfort* and has also joined his famous dad onstage on a couple occasions, including a 2021 homecoming gig at Fenway Park, to sing "This One's For the Children." Both of Joey's boys also did a special edition of "Spilling the ET" for *Entertainment Tonight*, in which they dished on their favorite NKOTB songs. For Griffin, it's "Single," while Rhys loves "The Whisper" and "Please Don't Go Girl."

Jonathan was the final New Kid to become a married man, wedding his long-time partner Harley Rodriguez in 2022, after years of hiding his sexual identity out of fear it would damage the New Kids career. "It's great. We've been together 14 years. It's nice to find love. We found each other later on in life, which makes it even better. We both understand each other," the singer told *Out* magazine.

Harley, who is a personal trainer, first met Jonathan in 2008 through a mutual friend and they had been engaged since 2016; Jonathan popped the question while the couple was on an African safari. They were even once contestants on a season of competition show *The Amazing Race*. In a 2023 episode of NSYNCer Lance Bass' podcast *Frosted Tips*, Jonathan spoke of the struggles he and Harley have faced in wanting to start their own family. "We tried it . . . It just didn't happen for us," Jonathan candidly shared.

Jonathan with then-partner, now-husband Harley Rodriguez in 2009.

"The theater community is important to me.
I'm cut from that cloth. I'm glad I've continued
to do some work in theater."

–Joey speaking to WFPK in 2022

Joey stars in *tick, tick… BOOM!*
in Boston in 2003.

CHAPTER TWENTY

BROADWAY COMES CALLING

All the world continued to be a stage for Joey once New Kids On The Block took their final curtain call. In a career pinch hit, Joey returned to his roots as a theater kid, taking his first post-NKOTB gig as Jonathan in a 2001 off-Broadway production of *tick, tick... BOOM!* (a show about an aspiring composer, so kind of a natural fit). It was staged at New York's Jane Street Theatre, with Joey continuing the role through 2003.

"The producer saw me in *People* magazine and they were trying to keep the show open," Joey told Kyle Meredith of Louisville NPR station WFPK, on being cast to be another familiar face (it also starred actress Molly Ringwald) and help draw an audience. The production opened just weeks after the September 11 terrorist attacks, when theatergoers were understandably slow to

come back to the theater. "The idea is to surprise people, you get the opportunity but then you show them you belong. That was a wonderful experience." Joey also recalled that time of his life to *Playbill*, sharing that playing the role of Jonathan "changed my life."

Joey was literally born for the stage. As the *Playbill* for *tick, tick... BOOM!* shares,

Joey's pregnant mother, Katherine, "carried" him to his first production in *40 Carrots* at the indie Footlight Club in Boston; as a child, he was a regular in the ensemble of Boston's Neighborhood Children's Theater. He appeared in dozens of shows before being poached by Mary Alford and Maurice Starr for the burgeoning New Kids On The Block project.

After receiving rave reviews for *tick, tick… BOOM!* in 2001, Joey was then cast to play Fiyero in *Wicked* in 2004, replacing actor Norbert Leo Butz and sharing the stage with Idina Menzel. The production, which he remained in through 2005, marked his official Broadway debut.

"He's very charming, very musical, and a much better actor than people who just know him from his pop group days may realize," said a report in *Playbill* at the time.

After *Wicked* came a role playing The Fonz in a production of *Happy Days* that debuted at Los Angeles' Falcon Theatre. The musical was directed by the TV show creator Garry Marshall and ran for a month in early 2006.

Upon NKOTB's reunion in 2008, Joey put Broadway on the backburner as he focused once again on his career with the resurrected music project. Then, in 2013, he starred in a one-man play called *The Kid*, based on his own coming-of-age story. It ran at the Garner Galleria Theatre in Denver and featured music from New Kids On The Block as well as the musical *Oliver!*, which Joey starred in as a young actor in Boston's community theater program.

"I've been doing this for as long as I can remember. And, frankly, I could get up and sing songs for the rest of my life, but I wanted to tell a story," he told the *Boston Globe*.

By the 2010s, Joey was in his stride balancing both the responsibilities of NKOTB and the Great White Way. In 2017, he got the starring role in the Steven Sondheim production, *A Funny Thing Happened on the Way to the Forum* at the newly renamed Garry Marshall Theatre in Los Angeles, a role that felt full circle: "Coincidentally, my earliest memory of the theater was *A Funny Thing Happened on the Way to the Forum*. . . . My mother and sister were in the show. The actor who played Pseudolus had this can of peanuts, and when he opened it, snakes would jump out. My friend and I would sit in the front row. My first job in theater was to collect the snakes."

After the 2017 production wrapped, Joey and his family moved from Los Angeles back to New York so he could pursue more theater opportunities. In 2018, Joey did a short stint in a regional production of *Cabaret* before he found himself back on Broadway in 2019, starring as Dr. Pomatter in the hit musical *Waitress*, based on the film and written by

Joey with Idina Menzel after their last performance in *Wicked* on Broadway in 2005.

Joey during his debut bows in *Waitress* on Broadway in 2019.

pop singer Sara Bareilles. It was a grueling schedule, but as Joey told *People*, "One of the benefits of having eight shows a week is that I always get another crack at it. Each show, I learn more about me and my character. So, I go back to the drawing board and come out next time, hopefully a little better, and just experience it again."

Most recently, Joey has appeared in productions of Shakespeare's *Twelfth Night* (2020); *The Wanderer* (2022), based on the story of Rock & Roll Hall of Famer Dion DiMucci; and *DRAG: The Musical* (2022), which details rival drag clubs and their will to survive in the modern landscape.

There are likely more marquees for Joey's name in the future. As he told *Boston.com*, "Career-wise, tops on my list is to do more theater. Not to be dramatic, but on my deathbed . . . do I want to say that I did theater and did enough theater? Absolutely. And I want to do it while I'm quote-unquote 'young.'"

BOY BAND TO BROADWAY

In addition to Joey, several other boy band alums have taken their turns on the stage in various musicals. It's a natural pipeline of talent, after all—being in a boy band requires knowing how to sing, dance, and even ham it up for the fans in the audience. In the case of a couple stars, they even got their start under Broadway's bright lights before joining music projects. Here are some of the pop icons turned *Playbill* stars:

Joey Fatone: The NSYNC member hit Broadway around the same time as the other Joey, first appearing in *Rent* in 2002 (below) and *Little Shop of Horrors* in 2004. Later casting included roles in regional shows like *The Producers* and *42nd Street*, as well as *Rock Of Ages*. He told the *New York Times* in 2004 of the differences between the two types of stages he's performed on: "Broadway is more intimate. But when you're at a concert, the energy is fun. I get a kick out of that."

Drew Lachey: After cutting his teeth in 98 Degrees along with his brother Nick, Drew was cast in several productions on Broadway, including taking on the role of Mark Cohen in *Rent* in 2005 and Patsy in *Monty Python's Spamalot* in 2008. In 2010, he was cast as Corny Collins in a production of *Hairspray* off-Broadway. Drew told *The Gazette*, "Doing Broadway, to me, is the top, to be around so many incredibly talented people that give so much to their craft and I have so much respect for."

Kevin Richardson: The Backstreet Boy got his turn on Broadway in 2003, when he was cast as lawyer Billy Flynn in the musical *Chicago* (above), replacing actor Billy Zane. *Billboard* notes he also had experience in regional theater before making his Broadway debut. Kevin stuck with the *Chicago* production for years. After wrapping up with the touring ensemble in 2003, he returned to the role in 2006 and 2007, and again in 2009, including staging the show in Japan.

....

Ashley Parker Angel: After making a name for himself in O-Town, Ashley took on the roles of Link Larkin in *Hairspray* and Fiyero in *Wicked* (the same role Joey McIntyre played). As he once told *Out* magazine, "I was all set to study theatre in college. As a teenager, I joined a small acting studio and I would have loved to have gone forward with that. But what happened was I got this audition for *Making the Band*, flew out to Las Vegas, and my career ended up going this whole other direction."

Nick Jonas: One-third of the Jonas Brothers, Nick was a breakout star on Broadway as a young child, taking on junior roles in productions of *Annie Get Your Gun*, *The Sound of Music*, *Beauty and the Beast*, and *A Christmas Carol*. As he matured, he returned to the Great White Way in 2010 when he was cast in *Les Misérables* as Marius and was nominated for a Tony Award for his performance (in 2003, he'd played Gavroche in the same show). In later years, Nick took on roles in *How to Succeed in Business Without Really Trying* in 2012 and *Chicken & Biscuits* in 2021 on Broadway, as well as playing Link Larkin in a one-off of *Hairspray* at the Hollywood Bowl in 2011.

....

Chris Trousdale: In the late '90s through the early 2000s, Chris was known as a member of Dream Street alongside Jesse McCartney. But before joining the boy band, he was a Broadway star, with roles such as Gavroche in *Les Misérables* and Friedrich von Trapp in *The Sound of Music*. Chris sadly passed away in 2020 at the young age of 34.

ROLL **CO6** SCENE **24A** TAKE **1**

C

04 07 22 07 LUT

EP: **1305** **BLUEBLOODS** DATE: 9/ 7 /2022

DIR: **ALEX ZAKRZEWSKI**

CBS 1/8

"I believe with acting, you play a role
when you're ready to play it."

—Donnie talking in a *Blue Bloods* roundtable in 2017

Donnie filming an episode
of *Blue Bloods* in 2022.

CHAPTER TWENTY-ONE

HEATING UP HOLLYWOOD

While Joey turned to Broadway after NKOTB's breakup, Donnie eyed Hollywood. By the late '90s, his brother Mark was already starting to become a household name, having starred in cult classics like *Fear* and *Boogie Nights*, and clearly Donnie wanted a piece of the action. In fact, he all but abandoned music to pursue acting—and it paid off handsomely.

"There came a point in my life where I got tired of doing the same old thing, and I knew I had to make a change and that's what I did," he told *Inside Edition*, who visited him on a movie set in 1997. But there was also a part of him that was looking for a deeper, more layered art form that might give him the respect he was craving, after growing tired of being the butt of jokes about being in a boy band.

"I started over . . . with a different goal for myself—not fame. Maybe it was respect," he told *Backstage* magazine in 1999. "One thing I learned through music was you can't make people respect you. In my music and singing career, I was famous and wealthy, but I had

no respect, at least not the type of respect I wanted or felt that I might have deserved."

Donnie didn't rely on his previous fame to break into TV and film. He did it the old-fashioned way, like any aspiring actor would: He relentlessly auditioned, and he dealt with lots of rejection—at least at first.

"I wanted to build, as opposed to trying to come in on the fourth floor and cheat my way in. So I got a small agent and hit the streets of New York and went to audition after audition and didn't get the part and didn't get the part," he told *Backstage*. Finally, in 1996, he got the role of kidnapper Cubby Barnes in the Mel Gibson-starring flick *Ransom*, directed by Ron Howard.

It also starred Gary Sinise, Lili Taylor, and Liev Schreiber. (To be transparent, *Ransom* was shot around the same time as Donnie's true debut in *Bullet*, which technically came out a smidge earlier but in a straight-to-video format—that film also starred Mickey Rourke and the rapper Tupac Shakur).

After finding success with *Ransom*, the late '90s presented Donnie with a multitude of acting offers, each role more complex than the last and allowing Donnie the chance to "hang tough" in a new way. In 1997's *Black Circle Boys*, Donnie played Greggo, part of a dark faction studying the occult; in 1998's *The Taking of Pelham One Two Three*, he plays NYC subway hostage-taker Mr. Grey; in 1998's *Body Count*, he plays would-be art museum thief Booker—curiously, the film was directed by Robert Patton-Spruill, who was a childhood friend of Donnie's back in Boston. The 1998 indie film *Southie*, shot on location in South Boston, also brought him back home. Donnie plays Danny Quinn, a recovering alcoholic who returns to his hometown and is lured back into a life of crime.

But it was the 1999 thriller *The Sixth Sense* that put Donnie on the map. In the gripping psychological blockbuster, Donnie plays Vincent Gray, a disturbed one-time patient of child therapist Malcolm Crowe (played by Bruce Willis). Vincent's harrowing storyline becomes a turning point for the film, which ultimately produces perhaps one of the greatest twists in all of cinematic history. The movie was also the breakout project of then-fledgling writer/director M. Night Shyamalan.

According to Donnie's biography on the CBS website, the network which airs his long-running TV series *Blue Bloods*, the part of Vincent Gray was actually written as a thirteen-year-old kid, "until [Donnie] met with M. Night Shyamalan to inquire about rights for a theater production and ended up convincing the writer/director that no one else but he could play the role." Donnie devoted himself to the part, losing thirty pounds by basically starving himself, alone, in a desolate New York apartment. By the time he appears on screen, he looks so vastly different, you wouldn't even know it was Donnie.

"I know it wasn't a huge role, but it afforded me the opportunity to challenge myself in a way that I had never been able to do," he told *Backstage* magazine. "Now I know simply that I can transform fully into

The poster for *The Sixth Sense*, in which Donnie plays Vincent Gray, a role that shot him to stardom.

LEFT: Donnie with his brother, Paul, at the Wahlburgers restaurant in Toronto in 2013.

RIGHT: Donnie with his brother, Mark, at the Los Angeles premiere of *Ransom*.

BELOW: The cast of *Southie* in Boston in 1999, from left to right: Robert Wahlberg, Jimmy Cummings, John Shea, Rose McGowan, and Donnie Wahlberg.

JOEY LOVES THE DRAMA, TOO

Although Donnie's acting career has been the most lucrative of the bunch, he's not the only New Kid to appear on both small and big screens. Joey parlayed his Broadway chops to character acting as well. He appeared in one season of the David E. Kelley drama *Boston Public* (below), about a high school in the city, on Fox in 2000, as well as the 2014–2015 CBS comedy *The McCarthys* about an Irish-Catholic sports family who, of course, live in Boston.

As mentioned, Donnie is also behind the scripted show *Return of The Mac*, loosely based on Joey's life and starring his real-life wife and kids (Donnie, Jenny McCarthy, and a couple NSYNCers appeared in episodes as well). Joey has also appeared in a few Hallmark Channel movies and had one-episode arcs on 2000s-era shows like *Psych*, *The Goldbergs*, *CSI: NY*, and *90210*, among others. He also appeared in a few films, including the 2004 movie adaptation of Broadway hit *Tony & Tina's Wedding*, the Sandra Bullock/Melissa McCarthy comedy *The Heat* in 2013, and *The Fantasticks* (based on an off-Broadway show) that came out in 2000.

The whole band has appeared in, or been paid tribute to, in other TV shows as well. Most recently, an episode of ABC's popular sitcom *The Goldbergs* paid homage to the New Kids in a 2015 episode entitled "DannyDonnieJoeyJonJordan," which featured characters recreating a "Hangin' Tough" dance video originally made by show creator Adam Goldberg. And in 2016, four-fifths of the NKOTB members appeared as themselves in an episode of Netflix hit *Fuller House* to wish DJ Tanner a happy birthday. That series builds off the *Full House* franchise, which was huge in the '80s and '90s, and had a Venn diagram crossover of fans with NKOTB. (In the episode, only Donnie was missing, though it was explained he was filming *Blue Bloods* in an apropos plug.)

Donnie in a scene from *Saw II* (2005).

another character, and I have the discipline that it takes. That's one of the reasons I had to jump on the role. I had to prove to myself, and to others that I'm worth being hired and that I can deliver."

The Sixth Sense was the second-highest-grossing film of 1999, and Donnie's standout performance pushed him to even greater opportunities in the new millennium. In the 2000s, he had a string of hits with the modern-day western *Bullfighter* in 2000; a movie adaptation of Stephen King's *Dreamcatcher* in 2003; the military saga *Annapolis* in 2006; Boston drama *What Doesn't Kill You* in 2008; and the 2000s-era *Saw* horror franchise, among others.

But it was TV where Donnie was really finding his footing in the 2000s. In addition to starring in the celebrated HBO World War II miniseries *Band Of Brothers* (2001), Donnie also found roles on NBC's multi-perspective detective series *Boomtown* (2002–2003) and of course ended up on CBS' *Blue Bloods* in 2010, where he played police officer and family man Danny Reagan until 2024, in his longest-running

role ever. In 2017, Donnie was nominated for Favorite TV Crime Drama Actor at the People's Choice Awards for his enduring work to play the character, which he has said is nearly a year-round job.

"One-hour dramas are so long. I pretty much work five days a week, sometimes 16 hours a day and eight months a year," he told *CBS This Morning*. "It's brutal hours but I worked my whole life to be in this position and I'm not going to complain about anything. I'm very grateful for all the opportunities I have, and I love what I do."

Donnie has also moved into executive producer roles, helming his family's A&E reality show *Wahlburgers* (2014–2019), as well as the reality shows involving his wife (*Donnie Loves Jenny*, which also ran on A&E 2015–2016) and band (*Rock This Boat* on Pop TV, also 2015–2016). He's also been behind the scenes for Joey McIntyre's 2017 scripted comedy series *Return Of The Mac* on Pop TV, the current HLN true crime show *Very Scary People*, and the 2013–2014 docuseries *Boston's Finest* on TNT, which follows the city's police force.

"I'm not worried about showing too much of our personal lives. It's only a slice of life, not my entire life. And I think it's good for people to get more of a sense of who we are and where we are from."

—Donnie talking to *USA Today* about *Wahlburgers* in 2014

Joey and Julianne Hough perform in the *Dancing with the Stars* tour in Florida in 2007.

CHAPTER TWENTY-TWO

GETTING REAL ON REALITY TV

In the '80s and '90s, fans went to desperate measures to get even the smallest glimpse of their New Kids crushes. They'd stalk hotel properties when the band came to town, hide in dumpsters outside concert venues, and even find out where the guys lived and set up daily vigils in the hopes they'd get a miracle sighting. "They're known all over the world and if you can even get a glimpse of them, that just brightens my day," said one fan interviewed by CBS Boston in vintage footage of a group that had assembled outside the Knight family home.

But by the 2000s, Donnie, Danny, Jordan, Jonathan, and Joey were basically open books, as they began their foray into televised docuseries, sharing *everything* with viewers on reality shows and winning over more fans on various competition series.

DANCING WITH THE STARS

Joey put his quick NKOTB moves to work on the first season of the popular ballroom dance-off show in 2005, where he was pitted against *Bachelorette* Trista Sutter, boxer Evander

Holyfield, model Rachel Hunter, game show host John O'Hurley, and *General Hospital* actress Kelly Monaco, who eventually won (Joey came in third place). Even so, it's not necessarily one of his proudest moments. "I like when people forget that I was on *Dancing with the Stars*, because the reality is that I did it because I didn't have anything else at the moment," he told *Boston Magazine* in 2021. "I was trying too hard, and forcing things. But I did get a lot out of it. You live and learn. And to each his own." As a coincidence, the reality show's host, Tom Bergeron, had actually crossed paths with Joey and New Kids On The Block years prior. Tom was a Bostonite who had his own morning show, *People Are Talking*, that aired on Boston TV station WBZ TV4; in 1989, the band appeared—with their moms—on the show for an in-depth discussion.

THE SURREAL LIFE

Jordan was tapped to be one of the "C-list" celebrities to take part in VH1's reality show, which makes a bunch of famous people live in a mansion together, take part in activities, and of course, stir up lots of drama. Jordan appeared in Season 3 of the show in 2004, which also starred *Full House* actor Dave Coulier, model/actress Brigitte Nielsen, *American Idol* alum Ryan Starr, rapper Flavor Flav (whom New Kids worked with on the 1991 American Music Awards telecast), and personality Charo. The most significant development was Brigitte and Flavor Flav beginning a relationship, though Jordan had his moments, specifically worrying about the lack of privacy in the beginning. The celebrities also headed into the studio to create a music track and did a performance with kids in the School of Rock. Jordan was invited back to the franchise for the *Surreal Life* offshoot

called *Fame Games* in 2006, in which former participants fight for a $100,000 prize, though he left in the first episode—calling his brother Jonathan to come get him—after learning their grandmother had died.

AMERICAN JUNIORS

It was promoted as *American Idol* for kids, so who better to judge the singing competition series than a New Kid who had been there, done that? That's exactly what producers had in mind when they brought on Jordan to be a guest judge on the show in 2003, where he was joined by singers Gladys Knight and long-time NKOTB cohort Debbie Gibson on the judging panel (former *Idol* Season 1 runner-up Justin Guarini was also a judge). Unfortunately, nothing really came of the series; it was canceled after one season and the winning combo of kid stars eventually disbanded.

TRUE LIFE

MTV's docu-series profiled real people with various struggles and followed them in their journey to self-help. One of those featured during the 2011 season was twenty-four-year-old New Yorker Frank, who struggled with panic attacks and anxiety disorder. Of course, it was the same condition Jonathan struggled with and partly led to the demise of NKOTB. So, MTV producers called on the singer to give Frank advice on how to manage his condition. In fact, Frank found great success in overcoming his anxiety and even started his own music artist management company. At the end of the episode, he is seen visiting the New Kids and hugging them backstage. In a follow-up interview with MTV, Frank explained, "I haven't spoken with Jonathan Knight too much. I'm sure he's very busy with the joint venture of the New Kids on the Block and Backstreet Boys. Jon is one [of] the nicest guys I've met and I appreciate all he's done to help me out."

THE AMAZING RACE

In 2015, Jonathan and his partner (now husband) Harley Rodriguez were one of the pairs competing on the CBS adventure series in which participants travel around the world, field clues, engage in challenges, and interact with locals in various countries in order to make it to the finish line and win a $1 million prize (the couple came in ninth place during their season). Jonathan told *Entertainment Tonight* that being on the show actually helped his panic disorder and made him more comfortable stepping up to the mic when he was on stage. "That was

one of the main reasons I did it, just to prove to myself I could. Being in a group with five guys, it was always easy for me to fall behind or to not speak up in interviews," he said, as Harley added, "He's a new man."

FARMHOUSE FIXER

Nowadays, Jonathan's reality TV time is taken up by this HGTV renovation show, in which he and interior design partner Kristina Crestin return old New England farmhouses to their original beauty. Jonathan has been renovating and flipping houses since the mid-'90s, when it became a new career focus after leaving NKOTB, and yet he still tears up seeing the end results on the show. During the second season in 2022, Jonathan even worked

Jonathan on an HGTV panel to discuss his show, *Farmhouse Fixer*, in 2019.

with his extended family (including Jordan) on their own farmhouse and told *People*, "It was a little weird at first. I'm so used to doing things that are New Kids-related with my brother, but then, all of a sudden, we're talking about kitchen sinks and stuff. But it was pretty cool to have him and the family on the show." Jonathan's success on *Farmhouse Fixer* has also led to his casting on similar home renovation productions like *Barbie Dreamhouse Challenge* and *Rock the Block.*

DONNIE LOVES JENNY

After their whirlwind romance, which began in 2013, Donnie and now-wife Jenny McCarthy decided to document their love story for an A&E reality show. It premiered in early 2015 with an inside look at their nuptials. As *Boston Magazine* said at the time, the show is the "realest you'll see Donnie Wahlberg" with episodes that profile his close relationship with his mom, Alma; moving to the Chicago suburbs; and he and Jenny deciding whether or not to expand their family. The show lasted three seasons, with the last episode airing in April 2016—and somehow avoiding the big breakup that normally comes when couples decide to document their lives for all the world to see. "People keep saying like, celebrity couples all break up on reality shows," Donnie told *Access Hollywood,* conceding, "But reality shows do not break up couples, couples break up couples."

THE MASKED SINGER

In 2021, Donnie took on the role of Cluedle-Doo on *The Masked Singer*, a singing competition where talents are disguised in elaborate

Donnie and Jenny McCarthy discuss *Donnie Loves Jenny* in New York in March 2016.

HOMEMADE MOVIES

The New Kids were no strangers to filming and baring all by the time they started exploring reality TV opportunities in the new millennium. Back in the '80s and '90s, they were the subjects of several very well-received VHS tapes that were some of the biggest sellers of their time.

The collection started with the *Hangin' Tough* tape in 1989, directed by long-time music video collaborator Doug Nichol, who was nominated for a Grammy for his work on the piece. The thirty-minute tape was released in July 1989 and featured the music videos for "Please Don't Go Girl," "You Got It (The Right Stuff)," "I'll Be Loving You (Forever)," and "Hangin' Tough," as well as many intimate moments behind the scenes while the band was on tour (below). Four months later, in November 1989, the *Hangin' Tough Live* tape was released, which presented a concert film showing NKOTB on stage at Los Angeles' Mayan Theatre. The two tapes were certified 11x and 12x platinum respectively, selling millions of copies together.

Several more tapes followed, including 1990's *Step By Step* VHS tape, which again combined music videos and live performances from the era. By 2010, NKOTB returned to the documentary-style format with *New Kids On The Block: Coming Home*, which profiled their comeback, the making of *The Block*, and the 2009 tour. It was released on DVD this time around, and was described as a "love letter to the fans."

Donnie, unmasked, with host Nick Cannon on *The Masked Singer* in 2021.

ROCK THIS BOAT

All five NKOTB members were part of this two-season reality series on Pop TV that documented their high seas adventure aboard the annual New Kids fan cruise. In addition to interviews and footage of the Kids themselves, many of those on board were also highlighted through their personal stories and attachment to the band. "Every year my bandmates and I go on a cruise with 3,000 of our wildest and most adoring fans," Donnie says in the intro to the first episode, which debuted in January 2015. "For the first time ever, we're going to take you behind the scenes to see what it's like. . . . Three thousand fans, 20 cameras, that equals a whole lot of potential chaos." There were live performances, costume contests, weddings onboard, Donnie's mission to break a world record for selfies, and even moving moments, like when Danny had a heart-to-heart with his kids about his late mom, Betty.

WAHLBURGERS

One of the most successful reality TV series that the New Kids participated in was the long-running A&E show *Wahlburgers*. It documented the lives of the Wahlberg siblings (particularly elder brother Paul, who's the culinary genius behind the operation) and their mom Alma, and showcased their attempts to grow their hamburger chain business. The series aired for 10 seasons from 2014–2019. "It's been an amazing journey that has brought us closer together as a family and launched our little business to heights we never could've imagined," Donnie said in a press release announcing the news that the show was ending.

costumes until they are eliminated and can reveal who they actually are. Jenny McCarthy is a judge, but she didn't find out her husband was behind the character until the rest of the world did. As the show's executive producer Craig Plestis told *Entertainment Weekly*, "I thought, 'Maybe we can get him, and I'll do it on the side, and not let his wife know.' . . . So, I called him up, and he said yes. And that was the moment like, 'Oh my god, how do we do this, how do we pull it off?' But she had no idea. He kept it completely secret. It was just a triumph. And in fact, there were times where he was calling her, she didn't even know he was in town at that time."

True to his testament, what grew from a single dining spot in Hingham, Massachusetts, in 2011 has now grown to a fifty-two-location, international empire, with restaurants as far as Australia and of course in their hometown of Dorchester. As of today, their brand of sauces are available in retail stores and Wahlburgers became the official burger of the Bostonites' beloved Red Sox baseball team in 2022.

But the real success of *Wahlburgers* came from how much it brought the often-fractured family back together, says Donnie, telling *Entertainment Tonight* the clan "came away from it for the better." As he shared, their mom Alma (who passed away in 2021) was able to find a new purpose for her life after raising her large brood, and also found a way to deal with the grief of losing daughter Debbie in 2003. And it allowed the brothers Wahlberg the chance to reconnect and "spend quality time together."

"Mark and I hadn't worked together since the Marky Mark days when I was his music producer and essentially his boss, and this really gave us a chance to spend time together both on camera and off," Donnie told *ET*. "I think it reminded Mark of my experience creatively. He started depending on me as a producer to be creative on the show and oversee editing while working with me on other restaurant stuff. It was a game-changer for us."

Wahlberg brother Paul at the Wahlburgers location in Hingham, Massachusetts.

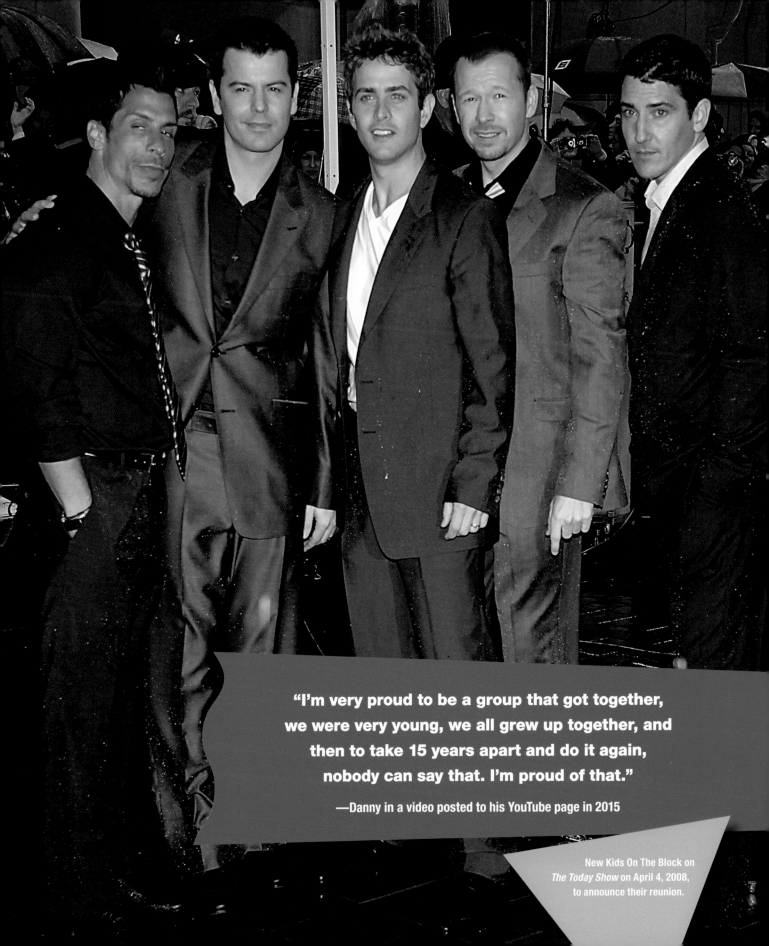

"I'm very proud to be a group that got together, we were very young, we all grew up together, and then to take 15 years apart and do it again, nobody can say that. I'm proud of that."

—Danny in a video posted to his YouTube page in 2015

New Kids On The Block on *The Today Show* on April 4, 2008, to announce their reunion.

CHAPTER TWENTY-THREE

FINALLY. . . THE BAND IS BACK TOGETHER

Rumors had been building for months about a reunion of NKOTB. And then the article on *People.com* on January 26, 2008, declared that Donnie, Danny, Jordan, Jonathan, and Joey were "back together" and ready to "stage a comeback"—all of it coming from a "well-placed source."

The article gave few details but pointed to the official website (www.NKOTB.com), which had been blacked out and unavailable for some time, but suddenly was active again, with a "television graphic with fuzzy, flickering photos of NKOTB in their heyday, and a link inviting fans to sign up for info." There was also streaming audio of a new track.

Things only got more confusing when Danny posted on his MySpace page shortly thereafter that it was all some kind of hoax: "I wanted to address the rumors of the NKOTB Reunion Tour. There has been no talk of this and you are getting it from [the] source directly. Never say never, and you can't believe everything you read," he shared, while also plugging his own new album.

NKOTB perform on *The Today Show* in May 2008.

Fans wondered what was going on—was it all a lie? Was the usually reliable *People* magazine (who had covered the band for years) wrong? Was Danny fired? Or was Danny just trying to drum up the suspense? On January 29, Danny's social media profile carried a new message: "I wanted to clarify since my first post this morning regarding the NKOTB reunion. I loved being a part of the group, and have always thought 'maybe someday we'll get back together'—you just never know when your someday will come. I can guarantee all the fans that if this reunion were to happen, they would hear about it first on www.NKOTB.com."

The website Danny directed everyone to now populated with a message all but confirming speculation. A gallery of old photographs from their heyday appeared on the screen, followed by the words, "Millions await their return. Are you ready?"

The confusion only fueled interest (well-played, Danny) as several outlets ran with the news and fans clamored to sign up for the mailing list. "When you said you'd be loving us forever, was that a lie too, Danny? *Was it?!*" *Vulture* hilariously wrote in an article.

Finally, on April 4, 2008, *The Today Show* brought out all the members of NKOTB and they announced their reunion live on air, adding that it would include a new album and tour in the coming months. They also announced their return to *Today*'s plaza in New York on May 16 to perform live for the first time in fourteen years as part of *The Today Show*'s summer concert series.

"We weren't going to announce this yet, but the story leaked on *People.com*," Donnie said during the broadcast, noting the band had decided in August 2007 to get the wheels turning again, although they initially tried to keep it under wraps until the time was right. "We thought we'd better come out and let them know it's official."

In the *Today Show* appearance, the band also announced they had new material they were working on and would be sticking to the same tried-and-true choreography that made them famous. "We're going to dance, we're going to sing, we're going to do it all," Donnie said. The band also confirmed the New Kids On The Block name would be intact, even as all the guys were nearing their forties. "We're all kids at heart, so it's not going to change," Danny said. True to form, their latest releases, including cover art for the "Summertime" single and album art for albums *The Block* and *10*, as well as tour names and promo materials, all featured the full name of the band again for the first time since *Step By Step* in 1990.

Anyone who doubted the hunger for the comeback of New Kids On The Block were put in their place seeing the televised reaction to the *Today Show* announcement—fans camped out for two days after learning of the surprise appearance and slogged through the cold and downpours the day of, letting nothing rain on their celebratory parade. Some fans came from as far as Texas, California, and Illinois, according to MTV, who recalled them

"screaming unintelligible noises, screaming marriage proposals, screaming that they love Donnie, Joey, Jordan, Jonathan, and Danny, even after 14 years."

As one fan told the music channel, "You have no idea what this means to us, that they're all getting back together. We get to feel young again and have that good-time feeling—and of course, the hotness helps. My whole wall was plastered with their posters, and when my mom tore them down, I was so upset. I couldn't go to the concerts then, but my mom can't stop me now. I'm free!"

Rolling Stone also reported that the *Today Show* "caused mayhem," describing "a crush of fans decked out in NKOTB jean jackets and tour laminates screeching with delight . . . [as the] boy band was bombarded by rain-soaked women dressed like teens (many with their actual teenage daughters)."

Some wondered about the timing. But, truthfully, in the mid-2000s, there were already a number of giant bands that had reunited (among them, The Police, The Who, even a very short-lived Led Zeppelin). And the rest of the boy band nebula that had logged their time in the interim were starting to break apart, leaving a gaping hole for New Kids On The Block to fill.

ABC News opined that the New Kids might have been most motivated by another pop group's reformation. "The band's current plans may have been inspired by the ultra-profitable reunion of the Spice Girls, who embarked on a sold-out concert tour late last year [2007], even though some questioned if anyone wanted to see aging former teen idols headed toward their 40s singing saccharine, sweet love songs." In the story, *Rolling Stone* magazine's Anthony DeCurtis bit back at that claim, "The real question is, 'Does it matter if it's good?' I mean, people scoffed at the Spice Girls, but they came back and had a good showing."

The *Boston Globe* put it more bluntly: "The New Kids timed their reunion perfectly. They waited until their fans were old enough to have enough money to misbehave like kids again."

The year 2008 marked twenty years since NKOTB's breakout album *Hangin' Tough* was released in 1988, which might've stirred up old feelings for members—though Donnie said it was the prospect of *new* music that drew him to the reunion conversation. "I had no interest going out on a nostalgia tour and singing the same material," he told *Today*, adding, however, "We absolutely will do the old songs, for sure."

Entertainment Tonight also reported that the idea of a comeback "had been brewing for some time." Part of it was the band members' trust in their new manager, Jared Paul, and apparently the good feelings that came from joking around about things like a Hot Topic line of NKOTB products that had come out. All of that eventually developed into conversations about how a reunion might work.

The article also explains that, when Donnie's marriage to Kim Fey was on the rocks, he started to throw himself back into work, and one of the projects he took on was recording some demos from an artist by the name of Nasri Atweh, who shared legal representation with NKOTB. Once Donnie brought in some of the other New Kids to contribute, inevitably talk soon turned to their own future.

Some of the members admitted they'd had doubts. As Joey told *E!* in a 2008 special, "There was a point since we disbanded that I thought we'd never get back together." Jonathan also told *Entertainment Tonight*, "We all had different reservations, but we were able to express them, figure it out, and make it work

so that it was a phenomenal time again." As he said in another interview with the outlet, "The main thing was, we did it for us."

Soon enough, East Coast members of the band had moved in with Donnie in Los Angeles, where he set up a makeshift studio, and together, they laid out the beginning pieces of their new material. That eventually became their comeback album, *The Block*, released on September 2, 2008.

The album was put out on a new label as they left their long-time home at Columbia for Interscope, apparently all thanks to a proud Blockhead named Aimee Nadeau, who worked for the company. According to *Entertainment Tonight*, when she heard the rumors of NKOTB's reunion, she asked the band's new manager Jared for a meeting, and made the proper introductions to help get the band signed to the roster.

With thirteen tracks, *The Block* was a more refined album with a contemporary pop sound. It featured some of Nasri Atweh's material, while Donnie and Jordan wrote a good portion of new originals as well. Moroccan songwriter RedOne also helped out, as did Timbaland. There were also special guests across the LP, including Ne-Yo on the track "Single," The Pussycat Dolls and Teddy Riley on "Grown Man," Akon on "Put It On My Tab," and even fellow former Maurice Starr protégés New Edition on "Full Service."

And then there was Lady Gaga. She was still up-and-coming—remember, it was 2008—but she helped write "Full Service" and also scribed and sang on the song "Big Girl Now." As discussed, the members of NKOTB knew even back then that she was going to be a huge star.

"She would walk into the studio and have this air about her of being this huge celebrity

even back then," Jonathan told *ET*. "I was always thinking, 'Who is this girl? What is she all about?' She had this mystique to her that was so intriguing."

Lady Gaga also gushed about working with NKOTB in an interview with *Daily Star* in 2008, admitting, "Working with them is the most incredible experience. They are an amazing talent. It is going to be a good year for them—I have faith that they are really going to come back with a bang." The budding pop star would also join NKOTB on their comeback tour that lasted from 2008–2010, where she opened one leg of the trek and often performed the song "Big Girl Now" live with the group.

Like their previous tours, NKOTB worked to the grindstone on their latest trek. The 150-show road trip was known as New Kids On The Block Live in 2008, rebranded to the Full Service Tour throughout 2009, and finally, became the Casi-NO Tour for the final leg in 2010. Each segment had different openers—in addition to Lady Gaga, Natasha Bedingfield, Tami Chynn, Shontelle, JabbaWockeeZ, Colby O'Donis, and Jesse McCartney opened several dates. The tour notably returned

The New Kids visit *TRL* in September 2008 to promote *The Block*.

NKOTB to the stadiums and arenas of their prime (upgraded from the smaller theaters they were relegated to on the Face The Music Tour in 1994). The total gross revenue topped $35 million, with some dates, like the Allstate Arena in Rosemont, Illinois, and New York City's Radio City Music Hall, garnering over $1 million all on their own.

The group hit a snag, however, with the planned 2009 tour dates in Australia, canceling all of them due to poor sales that were blamed on the worldwide economic recession at the time. Still, NKOTB soldiered on, and the era of *The Block* proved incredibly fruitful for the reunited group. Following the big comeback tracks "Summertime" (which reached No. 36 on the *Billboard Hot 100)* and "Single," *The Block* went on to become another huge record in the band's cannon.

Upon its release in September 2008, it shot up to the No. 2 spot on the *Billboard 200* chart and sold 95,000 copies in its first week. It also spent a total of seventeen weeks in the industry sales spotlight, showing that, even with time away, the band was still capable of the same pull with fans. As the *Los Angeles Times* put it in their album review, "Believe it or not, though, they've got the right stuff."

NKOTB signs autographs for fans at Newbury Comics in Boston in June 2008.

WHAT THE CRITICS SAID:
THE BLOCK

In 2008, *The Block* and the New Kids On The Block Live concert tour proved the band was back in a big way—and not just with fans. Critics were starting to take notice, too, and gave them some of the most positive reviews of the band's career. Of course, there were still the naysayers. Here's what critics had to say:

"Perhaps the surest sign of the New Kids' maturity here is the surprising strength of most of the material. They've been around long enough to know what a hit sounds like, and they're wise enough to know that they don't have forever to rebuild a following."

—Mikael Wood, *Los Angeles Times* album review

"I thought the building was going to collapse. I was screaming. Everyone was screaming. When the opening bars of 'The Right Stuff' started playing, I was dancing like a fool, singing every word, no longer pretending that I hated the New Kids On The Block."

—Billy Baker, *Boston Globe* concert review

"[Donnie] Wahlberg, Jordan Knight, Jonathan Knight, Joey McIntyre, and Danny Wood showed they still have the synchronized dance moves, smoothly harmonized vocals, and seemingly boundless energy they did back in their heyday of the late '80s and early '90s."

—Brandy McDonnell, *The Oklahoman* concert review

"For a group touring primarily on the strength of nostalgia, New Kids On The Block have conspicuously few hits, maybe a dozen at best (intense ones, but still). So their most significant accomplishment on Tuesday was that they managed to keep an entire arena of fans standing for two hours."

—Jon Caramanica, *New York Times* concert review

"And really, who wasn't an old school fan? New Kids On The Block know they cemented their fan base years ago, and the fans have been hanging tough ever since."

—John Wenzel, *Denver Post* concert review

"The quintet has adopted the all-grown-up-so-take-me-seriously suit-and-tie style of former boy bander Justin Timberlake, and from the very first track, the understated Akon-assisted slow jam 'Click Click Click,' there's a decidedly more adult approach at play here."

—Sal Cinquemani, *Slant Magazine* album review

"While it's nice to have the New Kids back on the block after a decade and a half away, you walk away from this album feeling like maybe they should have spent some of that time off learning to craft better material."

—Mike Joseph, *PopMatters* album review

NEW KIDS
ON THE
BLOCK

Jonathan, Donnie, Jordan, Joey,
and Danny ring the closing bell at
the New York Stock Exchange in
May 2008.

LET'S TRY IT AGAIN

NKOTB onstage during the 2010 American Music Awards

"This cruise we do is an absolute love fest . . .
Cruises for a while were where people went to retire,
whether you were an artist or a person, but now
everyone's doing them and it's a big party."

—Joey speaking to CBS Boston about the NKOTB Cruise in 2016

Donnie, Danny, Jordan, Joey, and
Jonathan onboard the third NKOTB
Cruise in Miami in 2011.

CHAPTER TWENTY-FOUR

CRUISING ALONG

As NKOTB settled firmly into their renaissance period in the new millennium, they turned to new ventures to delight the ever-devoted fanbase that had continued to stick by them. And what better thank you than a multi-day cruise where the Fab Five were literally in the middle of 3,000 fans day and night, taking photos, performing shows, and maybe even meeting up at the buffet?

Of course, the chance to be up close and personal with their childhood idols was a huge draw for those who spent years watching from afar, whether in nosebleed concert seats or burning their eyes with repeated watches of their old VHS tapes. The first NKOTB Cruise in 2009 sold out almost immediately. It has continued to sail the high seas every year since then (except in 2020, when a virtual edition took over during COVID)—and it continues to sell out year after year, with waitlists of fans hoping for a cabin to open at the last minute.

"It's a lot of fun for mommies who need to cut loose," one repeat cruiser told *ABC News* in 2010, adding the best part is that you get to spend face time with the band, like getting hugs from members and sharing hot tubs. "You think you're going on this cruise and you're never going to see them, but they're out everywhere."

The five-day itinerary includes several days at sea with themed costume nights, concerts, beach parties, and even New Kids *Jeopardy!* One day is also spent at a docked destination—in 2023, the NKOTB Cruise went to Half Moon Cay in the Bahamas, for example—

where attendees can take part in a range of excursions from horseback riding to kayaking and bike tours.

The cost of admission isn't cheap, from just under $1,000 per person for "limited event access cabins" to $3,799 per person for the grand suite accommodations with a balcony. But fans are willing to shell out the money. As *San Diego Union-Tribune* put it, "The little girls who made the New Kids On The Block a boy band sensation in the late 1980s and early 1990s are all grown up, and now they've got disposable income."

In a 2018 review, the *Boston Globe* described the experience as more than just a nostalgia trip, however. "This is a ship full of very active Blockheads. The fans who never left, who wear T-shirts that read 'I still love the New Kids,' who argue in online forums and know every bit of gossip and know everything Joey McIntyre posts on Twitter, who go back to their rooms during downtime and watch the 24/7 New Kids television channel that is playing on the ship's cable system. I see tons of New Kids tattoos, including one woman with an elaborate image of Joey McIntyre covering her entire forearm. And they save their money, because this is not a cheap event, and they come on this cruise every year."

Joey described the cruise experience to *Boston Magazine* in 2021, saying, "We really go all in. We're crowd-surfing half an hour into the voyage. You have to buy into the ridiculousness of the situation, and we do. We go hardcore for four days and four nights, and we give them the time of their lives. Yes, it's crazy. Everybody wants a selfie, like every five seconds, but we're very open with everyone. They're extended family by now."

The New Kids pose before the launch of their inagural fan cruise in 2009.

The annual voyage even spurred a reality TV series documenting all the fun. *Rock This Boat* lived on the Pop TV network for two seasons, from 2015–2016, not just following NKOTB but also the fans who go all-out for the annual event. The ongoing popularity of the NKOTB Cruise in later years would also inspire the band to do a version "on land," hosting the first-ever fan convention at venues outside Chicago in 2023.

LEFT: Fans dressed to the nines on the 2011 cruise.

BELOW: Fans wait eagerly to board the third NKOTB cruise in 2011.

ALL ABOARD!

NKOTB aren't the only ones with a popular music cruise (below). It has become standard fare for many artists over the years, not to mention the multi-band-themed ships that have come along, including the Rock The Bells Cruise: A Hip-Hop Experience, Keeping The Blues Alive, the Emo's Not Dead Cruise, and Monsters Of Rock's heavy metal affair. Here are just some of the acts that have set sail:

Backstreet's Back At The Beach

Boyz II Men's The Love Cruise

Maxwell's Urban Hang Street Cruise

Rick Springfield & Friends Getaway

The Beach Boys Good Vibration Cruise

Lamb of God's Headbangers Boat

Creed's Summer of '99 Cruise

311 Caribbean Cruise

Paramore's Parahoy!

The **KISS** Kruise

Lynyrd Skynyrd's Simple Man Cruise

Flogging Molly's Salted Dog Cruise

Kid Rock's Chillin' The Most Cruise

Train's Sail Across The Sun Cruise

Runaway to Paradise with **Bon Jovi**

"What he must've went through, back in the day, being in a boy band, and if there was a peep of him being gay, who knows? It could've shut down the group, been in tabloids. And now it's a plus, it's a bonus, it's a beautiful thing that he's out and he feels good."

—Jordan speaking to *Entertainment Tonight* about his brother in 2015

Jonathan performs on

CHAPTER TWENTY-FIVE

JONATHAN'S COMING OUT

The NKOTB reunion had barely begun when another unexpected twist came about—it was revealed that Jonathan Knight was gay. It's not that Jonathan ever hid his identity, at least not from his inner circle, who all knew. But there was a mentality of trying to protect the "image" of the boy band during their prime in the late '80s and early '90s that kept his truth from fans and the wider public.

To provide some context, the US was deep in the AIDS epidemic at the height of New Kids' fame. Not only that but, for a long time, the epidemic was referred to as the "gay plague" as it ravaged the LGBTQ+ community. Before there was treatment, *NBC News* says, "politicians on both sides of the aisle were debating in earnest whether gay people should be quarantined." It was a tragic time in American history and being out and proud was not wholly accepted in the '90s, especially not if you were one of the members of the biggest band in the world.

"We've come such a long way since we were Kids; I had CBS [who owned Columbia Records], I had my manager, I had all these people like telling me you cannot let anybody know you're gay," Jonathan recalled to *Entertainment Tonight,* adding that the band's team, including Maurice Starr, told him, "If you let the world know you're gay, you're going to ruin your career, your manager's career, CBS is going to lose money on record sales. It was just so much on my shoulders as a young kid."

That pressure, he said, led to panic attacks and stage fright, and ultimately led him to

Jonathan and Tiffany in October 1989.

an episode of *Watch What Happens Live* with Andy Cohen. She was asked for any sordid details about hookups with the New Kids, and responded, "The quiet one, the shy one. [He] became gay later. I didn't do it. I had issues with that. I was thinking maybe I did. Now looking back when we were dating, he was so much fun. We used to do facials together. He was so easy to talk to."

She later apologized on Twitter, after some backlash for revealing the information about Jonathan, posting on her social media, "Really didn't know that was the wrong thing to say . . . Never meant to hurt Jon." Jonathan responded to the Tweet and stepped in to defend her against the haters: "Tiff, please don't lose any sleep over it! I know you weren't being mean and I found it to be funny!"

There was no official "statement" from Jonathan or the NKOTB camp, but he did write a post on NKOTB's members-only blog at the time, as picked up by *Billboard*. In part, it read, "I love living my life being open and honest, but at this time I choose not to discuss my private life any further! My fellow band members don't discuss their private lives with their loved ones and I don't feel that just because I am gay, I should have to discuss mine!"

Still, the inroads that have been made when it comes to acceptance of the LGBTQ+ community in pop culture is something Jonathan is very happy to see, noting how at awards shows now, "no one flinches" when someone thanks their partner in their acceptance speech. As he told *Entertainment Tonight,* "If we were then where we are today, I would have been openly gay from day one with the New Kids and it wouldn't have been an issue. Back then there was such a stigma that I couldn't even tell my best friend."

decide to be the first to leave NKOTB in 1994, ahead of the band's official amicable breakup.

Even as the band eyed their reunion, Jonathan was still in the closet—and it gave him more trepidation about going back into the fame hamster wheel while keeping this part of his life secret. "It was scary for me to go back into the spotlight knowing that I hadn't officially come out yet. That was a big worry for me—it was scary to have to address it publicly and have prying eyes on me," he told *Entertainment Tonight* in 2018. "And, it turned out to be [a valid concern] because during rehearsals I'd be out on a date with [now husband] Harley, and we'd be spotted kissing in a restaurant and suddenly the blogs started and it was crazy."

In fact, it was a tabloid that first outed him after a former partner revealed all—with photos—to the *National Enquirer* in 2009, though it flew a bit under the radar. Two years later, however, pop star Tiffany (who once dated Jonathan very early on as the two toured together in the late '80s) broadcast the news even further when she let it slip on

HAPPILY EVER AFTER

Jonathan has since settled down with his long-time partner Harley Rodriguez (right), whom he married in secret in 2022. In fact, it was only because he was wearing a wedding ring during an interview with *Entertainment Tonight*, which prompted the journalist to ask him about the obvious jewelry, that Jonathan confirmed the news.

Jonathan and Harley originally met in 2008, as NKOTB was starting preparations for their reunion tour. Harley was working as a personal trainer and Jonathan would log time in his workout classes as a way to get to know his future husband.

"We were rehearsing the day I met him. He's a trainer at Barry's Bootcamp, so I would be with the band all day, then the only time I got to see him was to go take his class. . . . Then we'd go for dinner afterwards. He's been around from the beginning and seen [NKOTB's comeback] morph into what it is today," Jonathan told *Entertainment Tonight*.

Jonathan proposed to Harley during an African safari with their moms and friends in 2016 after tempting fate with wildlife and steep waterfalls. Though the two had talked about planning an intimate wedding, COVID got in the way.

In the years since, they've taken each other's names (as seen on social media), and Jonathan has appeared on Lance Bass' podcast, *Frosted Tips*, to discuss his union with Harley.

"NKOTBSB, it's like another group. Every now and again we say, 'Hey, New Kids was fun, let's go do NKOTBSB' because that's our other band."

—Donnie talking to MTV in 2012

NKOTBSB perform in Toronto in 2011.

CHAPTER TWENTY-SIX

TWO BOY BANDS TEAM UP

When it comes to boy bands, New Kids On The Block have never made themselves out to be gatekeepers. In fact, in most interviews where the band is asked about their "competition," the term is generally scoffed at. NKOTB has taken on an attitude of "the more, the merrier."

Their 2019 song "Boys In The Band (Boy Band Anthem)" is a testament to this perspective. It pays homage to the many groups that have come before and after NKOTB, with namedrops for Boyz II Men, New Edition, 98 Degrees, O-Town, NSYNC, Jackson 5, and Menudo, among others.

As Donnie told *Entertainment Tonight* of the song, "I take pride in celebrating our journey and the journey of other boy bands."

So, it wasn't a total shock—though definitely a surprise—when New Kids On The Block laid out the welcome mat for Backstreet Boys to start

a collaboration in the 2010s. Talk of the possible partnership started building in August 2010, when the media caught on to the development. *Billboard* said the two bands were "close to signing a deal with Live Nation" to host a conjoined tour in 2011 while also working on a collaborative single ahead of the pop-concert-palooza.

As a source told the trade magazine at the time, "The idea is to recreate the boy band phenomenon. It will be the ultimate ladies' night out."

The idea started germinating when Backstreet Boys made an unannounced appearance at the New Kids' Casi-NO Tour stop at Radio City Music Hall in June 2010. It was the first time NKOTB performed at the legendary venue, and to help fete the event, Backstreet Boys (including everyone but Kevin Richardson, who had stepped aside in 2006) came out from behind a curtain to join in the festivities. The two acts delivered a massive duet of BSB's big hit, "I Want It That Way." BSB also stuck around to perform "Shape Of My Heart."

"I want to thank those guys right there, they are mentors," BSB's Brian Littrell told the cheering crowd. "Backstreet Boys have been 17 years strong because of real people like them."

In an interview with *Entertainment Tonight*, Brian explained that the idea of show-crashing came up when the two bands were touring

near each other during the summer of 2010, and an invitation was made to have BSB join NKOTB for part of the show in New York. "It was a magical moment [that] none of us will ever forget. Right after we performed together, everybody on Twitter and Facebook . . . it was everywhere that we were going on tour. So we started talking about it and we made it happen."

Donnie even tweeted after the gig, "As for TONIGHT'S Concert . . . BACKSTREET BOYS got my respect forever!"

Donnie also recalled the genesis of the idea to *Rolling Stone*, sharing the Radio City Music Hall union "caused such a stir and we really got along with those guys. We said 'Hey, let's look into a co-headlining show.'" He explained that, at first, it was suggested that Backstreet Boys might open a series of dates for the New Kids,

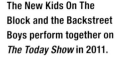

The New Kids On The Block and the Backstreet Boys perform together on *The Today Show* in 2011.

but Donnie thought that was "ridiculous . . . I didn't even want to insult them with that offer."

Instead, they took things even a step further than just teaming up, forming the ultimate boy band supergroup and merging their monikers to become NKOTBSB. Shortly after making an official announcement of the project and tour during *On Air with Ryan Seacrest* in early November 2010, the nine-member group gave a taste of their potential for the first time at the 38th Annual American Music Awards a few weeks later, performing a medley of each group's respective big hits, including Backstreet Boys' "Everybody (Backstreet's Back)," "I Want It That Way," and "Larger Than Life," as well as New Kids' "Hangin' Tough," "Step By Step," and "You Got It (The Right Stuff)."

It was a performance that was "surprisingly well executed," according to the *Denver Post*, and it all but "saved" the AMAs, which the newspaper reports otherwise brought in the lowest viewership in its history. Tickets for the NKOTBSB Tour sold out in mere minutes after the show. The group followed up the AMAs with a performance on the perennial holiday variety show, *Dick Clark's New Year's Rockin' Eve*, alongside other heavy hitters of the era including Kesha, Jennifer Hudson, Train, and Avril Lavigne, that was just as well-received.

"The excitement of this is just a glimpse of what our upcoming tour will be," NKOTB shared when details of the New Year's booking was announced. As the clock struck midnight on January 1, 2011, it kicked off twelve months of

New Kids during an NKOTBSB concert at Fenway Park in 2011.

NKOTBSB performs in Liverpool, UK, in 2012.

NKOTBSB domination. In May 2011, NKOTBSB released their eponymous debut album. The album paired five classic hits from each act with two new original songs, "All In My Head" and "Don't Turn Out The Lights." There was an element of fan participation for the record as well; in March 2011, fans were asked to vote for the individual band hits they wanted to be included on the record. The final tally came in at 250,000 votes and settled on obvious song choices like NKOTB's "Step By Step," "You Got It (The Right Stuff)," "Please Don't Go Girl," "Hangin' Tough," and "I'll Be Loving You (Forever)" as well as BSB's "I Want It That Way," "Everybody (Backstreet's Back)," "As Long As You Love Me," "Larger Than Life," and "Quit Playing Games (With My Heart)." The *NKOTBSB* album, which also features a six-and-a-half-minute dual band mashup track, entered the *Billboard 200* chart at No. 7 and continued ranking for ten weeks.

Then came the co-headlining tour, beginning May 25, 2011, and running through June 3, 2012. Each band took turns on stage throughout the show and then came together to do a few mashups. This was also the first

time the Boston-bred New Kids played Fenway Park (they were feted for the occasion with introductions from Mark Wahlberg and then-mayor Thomas Menino).

Originally, only twenty-five dates were planned for the US, but it was such a popular draw, the American trek expanded to forty-one dates with *Rolling Stone* hailing it a "gigantic success." Altogether, the tour spanned eighty shows across fourteen countries.

"There were naysayers when the New Kids first re-formed in 2008 and there were naysayers for this [tour]," Donnie told *Rolling Stone*. "It's sort of vindicating after years of people thinking we were sort of a flash in the pan."

In their review of the concert at LA's Crypto.com Arena (previously Staples Center) in June 2011, *The Hollywood Reporter* commented on the appeal, saying "Overall, the night could be described as one big nostalgia fest, albeit one that surprisingly didn't feel dated."

The reviewer added, "The groups knew what the fans wanted—hit songs, flashes of skin, and some well-choreographed dance moves—and they more than delivered." That particular show also offered the return of

A LITTLE HELP
FROM THEIR FRIENDS

It wasn't just the NKOTBSB Tour that saw New Kids finding comradery with their contemporaries. All the US tours that NKOTB embarked on in the 2010s decade (and the most recent trek in 2022) featured supporting slots or co-headlining billing from more of the oldies but still goodies.

THE PACKAGE TOUR

LINEUP: New Kids On The Block, 98 Degrees, Boyz II Men

DATES: May–August 2013

FUN FACT: The tour was announced on an episode of *The View*, with all the bands coming to the stage to perform a cappella; it was also 98 Degrees' first tour in twelve years.

....

THE MAIN EVENT TOUR

LINEUP: New Kids On The Block, TLC, Nelly

DATES: May–July 2015

FUN Fact: The tour was announced on *Good Morning America*. The concerts had a boxing theme, where the bands performed within a 360-degree stage "ring" with premiere seating around the stage.

....

THE TOTAL PACKAGE TOUR

LINEUP: New Kids On The Block, Boyz II Men, Paula Abdul

DATES: May–July 2017

FUN **Fact:** The tour was announced on *The Today Show*; it marked Paula's first tour in twenty-five years.

MIXTAPE TOUR I

LINEUP: New Kids On The Block, Salt-N-Pepa, Naughty By Nature, Tiffany, Debbie Gibson

DATES: May–July 2019

FUN Fact: This tour was also announced on *The Today Show*; besides Tiffany and NKOTB, it was the first time the acts toured together. The production came after the New Kids released a song called "'80s Baby" featuring all five acts from the tour on the track.

....

MIXTAPE TOUR II (below)

LINEUP: New Kids On The Block, Salt-N-Pepa, Rick Astley, En Vogue

DATES: May–July 2022

FUN **Fact:** All the acts appeared on *The Kelly Clarkson Show* to celebrate the tour announcement; it featured the return of Salt-N-Pepa, as they received a Grammy Lifetime Achievement Award and a star on the Hollywood Walk of Fame.

The New Kids and the Backstreet Boys help America ring in the New Year, performing in New York on December 31, 2010.

BSB's Kevin Richardson for the first time in five years. His official return to the group was announced in 2012.

Industry magazines hailed the NKOTBSB Tour as one of the year's finest. In a 2011 mid-year report, it landed at No. 44 on *Pollstar*'s Top 50 Worldwide Music Tours list, having by then earned $10 million with just a couple months logged on the road. By the end of the year, *Billboard* put it at No. 8 on its Top 25 Tours list for 2011, noting the production netted around $76 million as December rolled around.

Though NKOTBSB has yet to release another album, the bands have an "open relationship," according to Joey, who told MTV in 2012, "This door is wide open, our relationship is like a barn door. It's just blown

to pieces," and adding, "We had too much fun and we wish them the best."

The joint venture did have some legs in future years, at least as far as Jordan Knight and Nick Carter were concerned. In 2014, the two teamed up as a new duo dubbed Nick & Knight, announcing the project on *Good Morning America* and releasing one album to date in September of that year. They then embarked on an intimate theater tour that ran through November.

As Nick told *Time* magazine, the idea popped up during the NKOTBSB Tour. "When we were on tour, we both had solo records out and talked about doing a tour together with him singing his songs, me singing my songs. We stayed in touch and talked about that idea, and then realized that a fresher

idea that would be more exciting for both of us was to do a record together. We wanted to do something new for the fans, and fresh and exciting for us."

Detroit News called the duo's debut a "breezy album of adult pop and R&B that doesn't stray far from the two stars' comfort zones," while *Billboard* declares, "The notion that fans' appetite for boy bands of yore is not only alive but downright lusty was borne out most effectively by the 2011 project NKOTBSB . . . Nick & Knight, the new project of NKOTB's Jordan Knight and BSB's Nick Carter, distills that idea even further: What if a pair containing one member of each group did the same? The duo's peppy self-titled debut proves that the concept can not only work but occasionally triumph."

Nick & Knight was partly written by Nick and Jordan, though they brought in some studio help, including the noted production team the Stereotypes (Jonathan Yip, Jeremy Reeves, Ray Romulus, and Ray Charles McCullough II) who worked on the single "One More Time." Bruno Mars gets a writing credit on the song "Switch." The album entered the *Billboard 200* album chart at No. 24.

As Jordan told *Time*, he and Nick believed there was a fanbase out there for it beyond just the diehards, and regardless, they enjoyed the process. "My philosophy is just move forward and whatever happens, happens. As long as we know we did a great job, that's enough. I think this album has potential to reach new fans. If that happens, that's amazing, we would love that. If it doesn't, that's cool too."

BSB joins NKOTB onstage at Radio City Music Hall in New York in June 2010, the start of a beautiful friendship.

"We're five guys that have been in the business forever now, and we know what we need to do and where we need to go more than anybody. More than our managers, more than any producers, more than anybody, we know what to do. We're the guys in control."

—Jordan speaking to *Entertainment Focus* in 2013

The New Kids perform in 2010 at the American Music Awards in Los Angeles.

CHAPTER TWENTY-SEVEN

THE BIG 10 AND FEELING THANKFUL

And then there was *10*. In 2013, in the midst of their hectic touring schedule, New Kids On The Block returned with another new album that April—it was their second record since reuniting, their seventh full-length album, and their tenth release total (when factoring in the additional compilation or remix albums they've issued).

There was something wholly different about *10*. For one, it was the first to be self-released. Rather than go the major label route as they had done for years, the New Kids took total control and put out the album on their own newly formed label, originally called The Block/Boston Five. (It has since changed names, with the imprint called NKOTB Music as of 2017, when NKOTB released their last official record to date, the *Thankful* EP.)

What's interesting is that *10* wasn't really a planned affair. As Danny told the *Boston Herald*

in 2013, "We did these town hall-type events last year, and the first question everyone had was, 'When's the new album coming?' We weren't even thinking [about a] new album until people asked for it."

Working on their own label—and with their own finances—also meant changes to their usual process, the most obvious being forgoing the carousel of special collaborations that appeared on *The Block* from the likes of Lady Gaga, Timbaland, The Pussycat Dolls, and Akon (most were labelmates on Interscope,

so the contracts were easy and the revenue potential was high).

"No guests, no guests—that's the name of the album, no guests allowed. Except for our fans," Joey jokingly told MTV in 2012 as the band was entering the studio to begin work on the record. Donnie added in the article that financials definitely came into play: "We really can't afford any guests. We have a low budget."

As Jordan further explained to *Entertainment Focus,* it was a back-to-basics approach: "This time around we have just stuck together and we're doing it all by ourselves." As he posited, that dynamic made the album have "more of a deeper musicality and more introspective songs."

The first taste of the album came with the initial single "Remix (I Like The)," which came out January 28, 2013. The band had teased the song's existence on ABC's *The View* the week before, when they appeared to briefly announce the new record. "Remix (I Like The)" was a true

departure for the band, a clap-along retro R&B/soul track along the lines of a Bruno Mars or Fitz & the Tantrums, and it featured Donnie in more of a sing-song vocal style (along with Joey, who was also on lead).

"Sonically, [the song] is sort of out there; it's more a fun song. It's a little more retro [and] it kicks the doors open," Donnie shared with MTV. "We haven't put an album out in five years, so we wanted to come back with something that had a lot of energy and spirit."

Donnie also explained to the outlet that the song espouses the idea of beauty coming from within (fully exemplified in the music video starring actress Artemis Pebdani of *Modern Family* and *It's Always Sunny In Philadelphia* fame). "It's about someone becoming at peace with their inner beauty," Donnie said. "Some people might hear the song and think it's obvious. . . . Maybe it's about a beautiful girl walking down the runway or a guy stopping and gawking at a beautiful girl, but it's about someone who feels beautiful with who they are and is willing to celebrate that for all the world to see."

A second single, the softer ballad called "The Whisper," came out in August 2013, accompanied by a music video featuring live takes from the Package Tour.

Though neither song tracked on the *Billboard Hot 100* chart, the entirety of the *10* album found its footing, coming in at No. 6 on the *Billboard 200* and selling 48,000 copies in its first seven days on sale. It only fell behind one other artist of their ilk: Justin Timberlake, whose album *The 20/20 Experience* was number one in April 2013. It was a bit behind the No. 2 spot of *The Block*, but still a solid Top 10 entry in the band's catalog and right up there with the likes of *Hangin' Tough* and *Step By Step.* They were even above top artists like Pink and Bruno Mars. The album brought in a new production

and songwriting team lead by Danish visionaries Deekay, who have also worked with Diddy, Jordin Sparks, and Jason Derulo.

Like many albums in the New Kids canon, *10* received mixed reviews. While *The Guardian* discredited the record's "muddle of mid-2000s electro . . . bubblegum-urban modelled on their early hits, and conveyor-belt ballads" and *Michigan Daily* called it a mediocre, C-effort ("Melody, production, and lyrics are as basic as can be. Each track is a hollow-shell version of the typical boy band music of the early 1990s"), *The Arts Desk* hailed "Remix (I Like The)" as "surprisingly fresh," and credited the album's "slick production." They added it was "an album long-timers would be proud to add to their collection." *Entertainment Weekly* also gave the album a B, noting its "breathy, elevator-ready ballads and jazzy uptempo ditties."

New Kids On The Block performs during a concert at the Amway Center in Orlando, Florida.

Reviews aside, the band had the most fun making *10* out of perhaps all the records in their career, embracing who they are and letting go of others' opinions. As Donnie told the *Huffington Post*, "I enjoy every aspect more now than as a kid—performing, recording, touring. I feel more at ease and confident, which is saying a lot because it's a young man's game."

To celebrate the album's release in April, the band performed a special gig at the iHeartRadio Theater in New York, which made headlines after Jonathan exited the stage without warning. As *The Hollywood Reporter* noted, "[Jonathan] appeared visibly uncomfortable on stage, and opted to stand behind his fellow bandmates . . . and answer text messages while the rest of the group executed their signature, synchronized choreography." The outlet also noted that the members of the band tried to comfort him with hugs while the audience sent "their own cheers of encouragement."

Many assumed Jonathan's past history with anxiety and stage fright might have been at play here. After the incident, he posted "I'm sorry . . ." on Twitter, without much more explanation. However, once the Package Tour kicked off May 31 of that year, there weren't any other reports of Jonathan struggling with being onstage.

The day before that tour kicked off, NKOTB also participated in the Boston Strong Concert at TD Garden to raise money for One Fund Boston, which helps those affected by the marathon bombings that occurred in April 2013. As *The Hollywood Reporter* shared, Joey, who took part in that year's running event, was emotional as he said to the large crowd, "I don't care where you were that day, because this happened to all of us."

After wrapping up the Package Tour and completing a trek in Europe the following year, the New Kids returned to the stage in the summer of 2014 with a mini-residency in Vegas to celebrate the thirtieth anniversary of the band. Called "New Kids On The Block: After Dark," it took place at the Axis Theater at Planet Hollywood from July 10–13, 2014 (the same spot where Britney Spears was doing her own concurrent residency).

As MTV reported at the time, it was a huge success, noting, "if the night was any indication, a full-on Vegas residency of their own wouldn't be a bad idea for the all-man boy band." In fact, Joey told the outlet the mini-residency was a "test run" and a way of "dipping our toe in" to the idea. They haven't returned to it since, but with Vegas residencies becoming a huge draw in the modern music landscape, it wouldn't be surprising if they announced one in the future.

The only other official release to come in this era and to date (besides non-album singles) was NKOTB's first-ever EP in May 2017. Called *Thankful*, it featured just five tracks, including the single "One More Night" and the title track, which the band said was directed at their fans and their years of dedication. A bonus track called "We Were Here" features DMX and was included on the version of the EP sold exclusively at Target stores. In December of that year, NKOTB released an expanded edition that included three more songs—all holiday themed: "Unwrap You," "One Night Of Peace," and "December Love." It was the band's first holiday music since 1989's *Merry, Merry Christmas*.

NEW KIDS GET THEIR STAR MOMENT

There was another reason for the band to be *Thankful* in this time period: They got their star on the Hollywood Walk of Fame in 2014, the 2,530th Star dedication on the famous Hollywood Boulevard.

A special ceremony was held October 9, 2014 (below), with a speech given by none other than Arsenio Hall, who had supported the act many times in their early days. "I love these guys, talented, classy guys. I love them as much as a Cavalier fan from Cleveland can love guys from Boston," Arsenio jokingly began his speech. "I got a cassette tape on my desk in 1984. (Some of you don't even know what that is.) And it was these guys and I've been a huge fan ever since. . . . You know why I love them? They make us happy. They really do. You can't listen to a song or watch a video and not smile. I dare you."

Arsenio then recalled his "favorite memory" of NKOTB regarding the lip-synching debacle, noting the band's "honor and their dignity is the most important thing to them." The former talk show host ended by saying, "These songs will be our oldies when we are old. We have the greatest oldies in the history of music because we have New Kids."

Donnie, flanked by his bandmates (all of whom were wearing suits decorated with a pink ribbon pin in honor of breast cancer survivors) came to the podium next, noting it was the first time the band was "collectively speechless" at the huge honor. He did eventually pull it together, thanking many on their team, including their first choreographer David Vaughan and of course Maurice Starr, both of whom were in the audience. Donnie also thanked the fans: "We wanted someone to share this journey with," he said, getting choked up. "Without you, it means nothing."

Of course, the singer also thanked his bandmates, sharing, "We've been together for pretty much 30 years. We've been friends for longer. We've been through the droughts of droughts, the highs of highs. We've been through things that most people could never imagine. We went from playing for food and meals in prisons and high schools and birthday parties and bar mitzvahs to playing for the most amazing fans in the world, all over the world. And I think I speak for all of us in saying that I would not have wanted to spend one moment of the last [thirty] years doing this with anyone besides this team right here."

New Kids On The Block perform at the Apollo Theater in New York on October 7, 2018, to celebrate the thirtieth anniversary of *Hangin' Tough*.

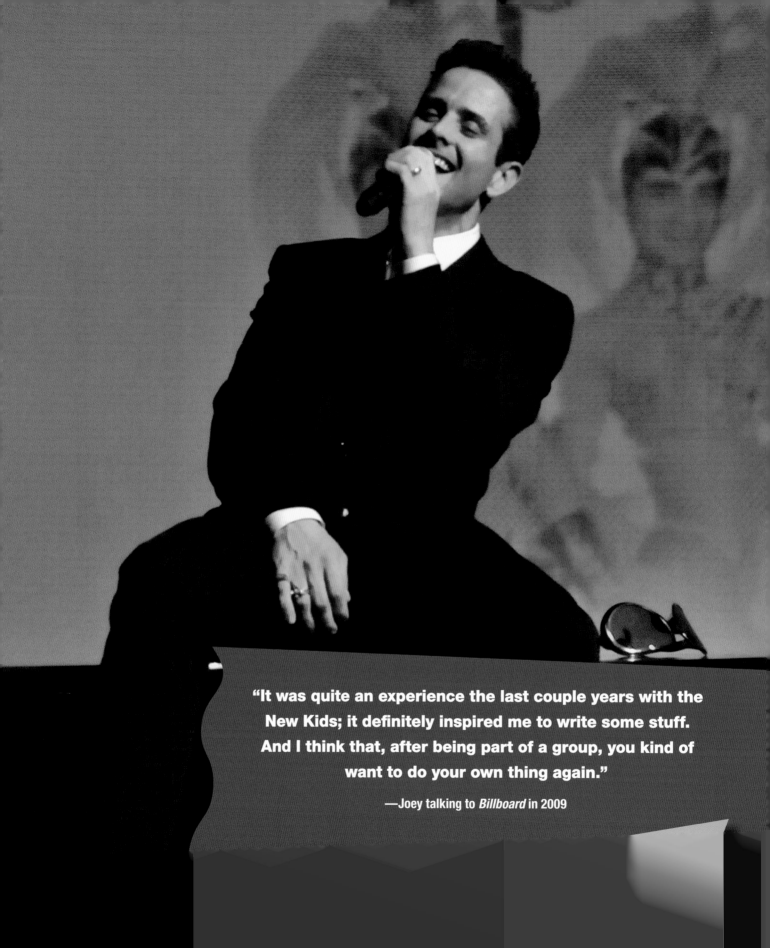

"It was quite an experience the last couple years with the New Kids; it definitely inspired me to write some stuff. And I think that, after being part of a group, you kind of want to do your own thing again."

—Joey talking to *Billboard* in 2009

CHAPTER TWENTY-EIGHT

AN ENCORE OF SOLO WORKS

Even after New Kids On The Block reunited in 2008, Joey, Jordan, and Danny continued to have their eye on solo works and remained prolific in this later era. Donnie and Jonathan stayed the course on their individual pursuits, as well, the former appearing in TV and movies and the latter continuing to work on his home renovation projects.

Following the one-man works Joey released in the interim years—*Stay The Same* (1999), *Meet Joe Mac* (2001), *One Too Many: Live From New York* (2002), *8:09* (2004), and *Talk To Me* (2006)—he came back strong in 2010 with the appropriately-titled *Here We Go Again* and followed it up in 2011 with a holiday album, *Come Home For Christmas*.

The seven-track *Here We Go Again* was advanced with the title track as a single and an accompanying music video that features a shirtless Joey in a *Fight Club*-esque match as a crowd cheers his victory. As Joey explained in a behind-the-scenes piece, it was an allusion to his career as a solo artist. "It's an ongoing fight and that's why the video has that theme of getting in the ring and going for and being able to take a few punches but being able to come back. Regardless of all that stuff, I still want to get up and take a swing at it and go for it."

The single and album didn't chart on *Billboard* like his debut *Stay The Same* had a

decade prior, but he did support the effort with some intimate club show dates; he also offered fans some special edition merch, including a "Mac Pac 3000 goodie bag" with a CD, booklet, and photos. "Every two or three years I just get itchy and I want to make a new record, and being out on the road and performing so much only encouraged me more," he told *Billboard* at the time, noting that he began work on *Here We Go Again* just two days after the New Kids reunion tour in 2009 wrapped.

True to his word about scratching the "itch" to make new music, *Come Home For Christmas* came out just a year later. As he told *Monsters & Critics* at the time, it was in the works for a while: "My Christmas album has always had a prominent place on the back burner." Across the fifteen tracks, there are a few duets that took on personal meaning.

His sister, Carol Gallagher, appears on "Do You Hear What I Hear?" Joey told *M&C,* "It was very special to sing with my sister. I would not have been where I am in my career without her first holding my hand and leading me on stage." There's also Jordan Knight, who appears with Joey on a mashup of "Peace On Earth/ Drummer Boy," and Joey's son Griffin even has a featured part on "The Chipmunk Song."

After the 2011 Christmas gift, Joey went quiet as far as solo works for the next decade. He picked it up again in the 2020s, releasing a few non-album singles, including "Own This Town" in 2020 and "Prolific" and "Lost In Your Eyes" in 2021. The latter is a take on Debbie Gibson's 1989 hit, this time done as a duet.

Nick Carter of the Backstreet Boys performs with Jordan in West Hollywood in 2014.

JOEY MAKES ANOTHER "MOVE"

In 2017, Joey ventured out into another endeavor, launching his own podcast, *The Move with Joey McIntyre*. It wasn't about music or even about Broadway—it was about people who had moved residences. It was something he was all too familiar with, having relocated from Boston to New York to Los Angeles on numerous occasions for various projects with which he was involved.

As he told *Boston Magazine*, "It was a way to share and connect with people about what I was going through when I moved to New York. . . . [And now] I'm moving back to LA. I thought of it as sort of like *Queer Eye* for people who are moving. Everybody's clueless, it seems. We all move at some point, but every time, we go, 'What do we do? How do we do this?'"

Only fourteen episodes were produced, with the series wrapping up in 2018 (it's still available on Apple, Spotify, Stitcher, and other audio streaming networks). His guests included actors Chet Dixon and Jimmy Dunn, athlete David Heath, and comic Adam Ray. His family also appeared in a New Year's Day episode in January 2018.

"He thought of it!" Debbie told *USA Today*. "When I was signed on to do the Mixtape Tour (in 2019 with New Kids On The Block), Joey called and asked how I would feel about duetting on the song, and I was like, 'Wow.' He had that vision. I honestly don't think I would have thought of it."

Joey also heralded Debbie as "someone who I admire and share so much history with" to *Entertainment Weekly*. The duo ended up doing their own mini-residency together in Vegas at the Venetian in August and September 2021.

Joey has continued to tour solo. As recently as 2023, he continued a mission he started in 2022 to do fifty shows to commemorate his fiftieth birthday. The trek included his debut at New York's famed Carnegie Hall in January 2023, which he told *People* was an emotional moment. To mark the milestone he invited Debbie Gibson, all the New Kids, and his colleagues from several Broadway productions to take the stage with him. Notably, he sang a Frank Sinatra song for the crowd, the same way he did for his initial audition for NKOTB in 1984. "To say I've come a long way feels like a crazy understatement. To be on stage at Carnegie all these years later, singing to a room filled with the love of friends, family, and fans. I'm just truly grateful for it all."

Jordan also had another solo album come out in May 2011 (of course, in addition to the

2014 album *Nick & Knight*, his collaborative project with Nick Carter). Jordan told *Billboard* the album, *Unfinished*, started out as a "hobby" more or less, but added, "The music started coming out so good, and I started talking to some record people and had the idea of doing a whole album." It also helped that the New Kids were on the road with NKOTBSB at the time, providing ample opportunity to promote the album and give it more exposure. Notably, *Unfinished* was released on Jordan's own label, JK Music. As *Contact Music* noted, JK Music is under the umbrella of Mass Appeal Entertainment, whose CEO, Marcus Siskind, has also worked with the Backstreet Boys.

Unfinished led off with the single "Let's Go Higher" on March 1, 2011, followed by the second single "Stingy" on June 29, the latter featuring Donnie in a guest spot. The album made its way to the *Billboard 200* chart, coming in at No. 48. The album tapped more into Jordan's "up-tempo pop roots," as he told the trade magazine, adding, "There's this idea that when you turn 40, you automatically go to adult contemporary heaven, but I want to try and challenge that. My heart has always been in more up-tempo music you can dance to."

Due to the NKOTBSB Tour, Jordan didn't host his own concerts upon his album's release, though he did do special one-offs in some of the markets where the mega-group played.

Danny has also so far put out one more solo album in the post-reunion era, January 2016's *Look At Me*. It was previewed with a pair of singles issued in 2015, including the title track and "Endlessly (Betty's Wish)," the latter an homage to his late mother. He did a brief tour in January 2016 with six East Coast dates and made two promo stops along the way, returning to the stage at *The Today Show* and appearing

on Jenny McCarthy's former SiriusXM program, where even Donnie showed up for the segment. In an Instagram post, Danny thanked the couple and said, "You both made me feel so proud today and your support means the world to me."

As Danny told *Billboard*, proceeds from the sales of *Look At Me* were donated to the Remember Betty foundation in an ongoing effort to support breast cancer patients and their families. He also told the magazine that, in addition to his mother, being a single father and raising his three kids highly informed the new material. "This record is definitely a reflection of the past ten years. The good and bad. My mother's foundation is a big inspiration in my writing. All the breast cancer patients that have passed away, survived, and the ones that are living with this disease. They all have inspired this record."

In an "A" review, *Digital Journal* said, "Danny Wood pours his heart out on this album, and many fans and listeners (and anybody who has ever lost a loved one) are able to relate. He is not afraid to showcase his vulnerability as a recording artist."

Nick & Knight perform in Vancouver, Canada, in 2014.

"Our fans have showed up for us for over 30 years. We really are a family at this point . . . I know what music means to me when I can put on the right song and it can just lift my heart and put a smile on my face. To know we do that for people is a real huge gift."

—Joey talking to CNN about NKOTB's pandemic-era song "House Party" in 2020

CHAPTER TWENTY-NINE

AN "ANTHEM" AND A "HOUSE PARTY"

As the 2010s were wrapping up, New Kids On The Block appeared once again on *Dick Clark's New Year's Rockin' Eve* on December 31, 2018, with a crowd of an estimated 1 million people live in New York. They were joined by musical guests Christina Aguilera, Dan + Shay, and Bastille, as well as Donnie's wife, Jenny McCarthy, who co-hosted the event with Ryan Seacrest. It would've been almost the perfect night, except for the pouring rain.

"It seems every time we're outside for a big performance, it's pouring," Donnie joked in an interview with *Variety*, of course recalling another big occasion when there was a massive downpour: their reunion announcement on *The Today Show* in 2008. "The fact that it's raining sort of stacks the deck against us, but that just brings us back to the early days, when everything was stacked against us," he added.

In fact, the televised New Year's Eve show from Times Square was just months after the New Kids celebrated their beginnings with a special thirtieth anniversary performance at the Apollo Theatre in Harlem that harkened back to the first time they played the hallowed hall in 1988. For all intents and purposes, the final night of 2018 marked a great ending to one chapter and a positive outlook to start a

NKOTB performs on *Dick Clark's Rockin' Eve* on December 31, 2018.

new one. As 2019 played out, it brought the first trek of the Mixtape Tour in May, where they were joined on the road by Salt-N-Pepa, Naughty By Nature, Tiffany, and Debbie Gibson (allowing Debbie and Joey to work together on the later "Lost In Your Eyes" duet).

The year also sparked a jovial new song from NKOTB with the nostalgic "Boys In The Band (Boy Band Anthem)," released on March 2. Not only did the track talk of the New Kids' roots but it also honored the many boy bands who came before and followed after. In the rap breakdown, Donnie names-drops the Jackson 5, the Osmonds, New Edition, Bell Biv DeVoe, Backstreet Boys, 98 Degrees, LFO, O-Town, NYSNC, and One Direction, among others, while indulging in a history that started in Motown and spread to various cities from Boston to Houston to Orlando. (The ethos of "Boys In The Band" also led to the "Battle of Boston" segment at the 2021 American Music Awards.)

The accompanying music video for "Boys In The Band (Boy Band Anthem)" was just as fun, starting off with Lance Bass posing as a teacher in a full high school classroom, announcing a special guest to talk about the history of boy bands. NKOTB appears in grandpa cardigans with walkers and canes, looking like they just came from the retirement home, to lead off the song (and prove they're never above poking fun at themselves). But soon they shed the visage and run through the looks and dance moves of each decade, from the '70s to the present day—including their own "Right Stuff" two-leg swing and NYSNC's "Bye Bye Bye" puppet moves. The visual piece also featured a number of cameos—in addition to Lance Bass, there was Debbie Gibson, Naughty By Nature, and Bell Biv DeVoe. The music video has since been viewed 15 million times.

Yet, like everyone else in the world, New Kids On The Block had to endure the trials of the COVID-19 pandemic in 2020. Though no tour dates were canceled—the first edition of the Mixtape Tour had wrapped in July 2019—the New Kids were still stuck at home. Wanting to connect with fans and give them something to smile about, NKOTB released the song "House Party" on April 24, 2020. At the beginning of the song, Donnie offers a heartfelt message, "For those about to lose their minds, we gotta remember that in the worst of times, we can make the best of times," before the beat kicks in.

"I was inspired. People need to be entertained, to feel light, to be happy. If we can do even the smallest thing to lift someone's day, we will do that," Donnie told *Billboard*. The song, which was written by him and producers Deekay via FaceTime, was meant to lift people up and maybe even get them motivated to create a dance party at home with their families.

Like "Boys In The Band (Boy Band Anthem)," the "House Party" video was also cameo-centric, featuring vocal parts from Boyz II Men, Naughty By Nature, Jordin Sparks, and Big Freedia. The accompanying music video featured all the contributing music stars in raw video from their own home studios; it also offered appearances from NKOTB's families, Jenny McCarthy, Mark Wahlberg, Kid 'n Play, Derek Hough, Carrie Underwood, Nicole Scherzinger, and actor Ken Jeong in self-filmed snippets that take on the feel of one big virtual Zoom party.

Proceeds from the song and part of the sales of special merch created for it were donated to the organization No Kid Hungry—and did quite well for the charity, since the song

A BIG HOMECOMING AT FENWAY

Once it was deemed safe to resume hosting live events, New Kids On The Block hit it out of the park with their next big concert—returning to their home turf at Boston's Fenway Park for the third time in their five-decade career (the first time being in 2011, below). The grand spectacle was pushed back twice due to COVID, originally set for September 2020 and then July 2021, but when it did finally happen on August 6, 2021, it was worth the wait. Throughout the night, they were joined by fellow Boston natives Bell Biv DeVoe (the group that grew out of the ashes of New Edition), as well as Joey's son Griffin McIntyre who helped his dad and co. on piano for "This One's For The Children."

The band, along with Live Nation and the Boston Red Sox, gave a good number of complimentary tickets to the city's first responders and health care workers to thank them for saving lives throughout the pandemic.

As *Boston Herald* reported in their review, the band hit a homerun from the moment the concert started: "NKOTB hit the stage to shrieks, shouts, cheers, and cries of joy. In tight white jeans and silver-sequined jackets with Sox-style 'Bs,' the five Boston heartthrobs slid through synchronized moves under a rain of confetti and bursts of fireworks. It was [just] the first song."

The paper also reported that the New Kids' concert was just one in a series the ballpark hosted since reopening their gates that August, following shows from Guns N' Roses, Billy Joel, Green Day, and Weezer, and conceded, "New Kids proved, over two epic hours and three dozen songs, they belong in that storied company."

The *Boston Globe* also positively reviewed the concert, hailing it a "high-energy homecoming."

reached the No. 5 spot on the *Billboard Digital Sales* chart.

"All we want to do is give back in the best way we know how," Donnie added in his chat with *Billboard*. The band also auctioned off the once-in-a-lifetime chance to spend a tour day with NKOTB once live events resumed, with those proceeds benefitting No Kid Hungry as well.

"We're all feeling nervous and scared and frustrated," Donnie told *Good Morning America* about the origin of the song. "And this is a chance to just let it all go and have a party."

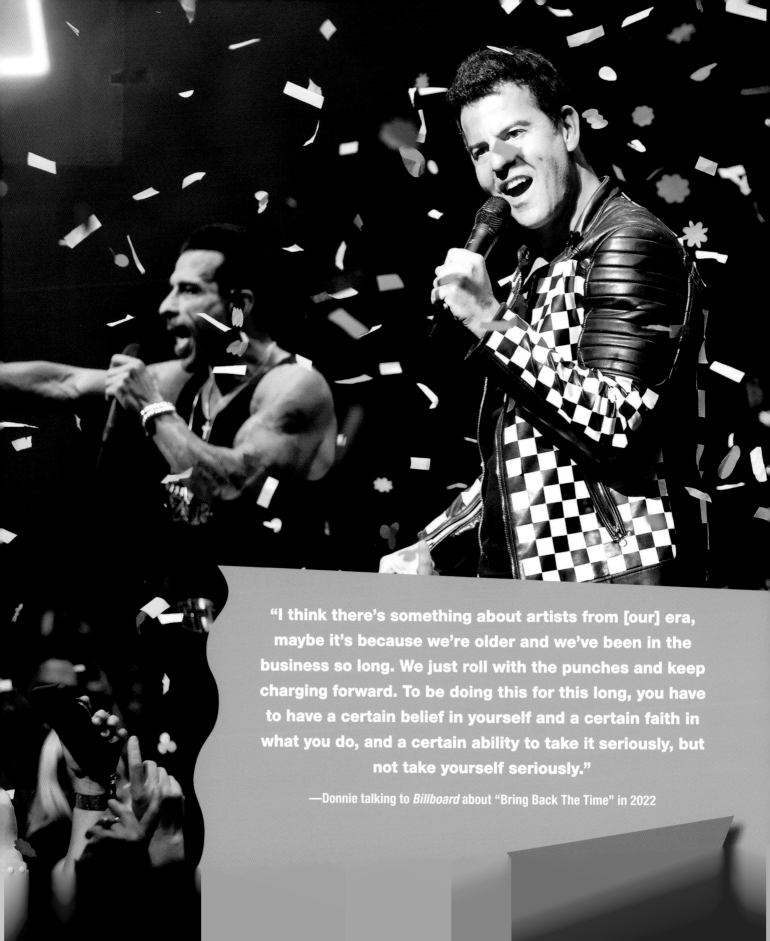

"I think there's something about artists from [our] era, maybe it's because we're older and we've been in the business so long. We just roll with the punches and keep charging forward. To be doing this for this long, you have to have a certain belief in yourself and a certain faith in what you do, and a certain ability to take it seriously, but not take yourself seriously."

—Donnie talking to *Billboard* about "Bring Back The Time" in 2022

CHAPTER THIRTY

LOOKING TO THE FUTURE

Post-reunion and post-pandemic lockdown, New Kids On The Block have still remained active. As Danny once pointed out, the band has been together longer in this second phase (16 years and counting) than they were originally from 1984 through the breakup in 1994. Part of the reason is they're simply having more fun this time around, and not feeling as much pressure.

"There's a maturity that we probably lacked the first time around, even though we kind of got into this when we were all young teenagers and had to mature very quickly. It all happened so fast, it was hard to appreciate it all. And I think with this second go-around, we're all just all so much more grateful for all of it," Donnie told the *Chicago Sun-Times* in 2023. "It's that age-old question, 'If you had the chance to do it over again, what would you do differently?' Well, we're doing it. We're living it out right now."

You can see the joy in their mashups for "Boys In The Band (Boy Band Anthem)" in 2019, and their latest, "Bring Back The Time," released in 2022. Another nostalgic anthem,

pining for the '80s heydays and attesting to the fact they're the same as they "were in '89," it once again sees NKOTB recruiting their contemporaries and tour mates, with guest vocals from Salt-N-Pepa, Rick Astley, and En Vogue (all of whom appeared on the second edition of the Mixtape Tour in 2022).

The music video is also a total throwback, with all the New Kids donning costumes and makeup to recreate videos of yore from the likes of Devo, Twisted Sister, Flock of Seagulls, Robert Palmer, Billy Idol, Talking Heads, and Duran Duran, among others. The video, which was directed by John Asher (Jenny McCarthy's ex-husband) has been viewed 5.3 million times and counting.

As Donnie told *Billboard*, "Every single artist was so excited to jump in and be a part of this song. It's an anthem. It's uplifting. It's fun and it's exactly what we could all use right now." Donnie added he worked on the track with current go-to producers Deekay the day after NKOTB played Fenway Park in 2021 and that it dovetails with New Kids' itch to make new music every few years.

The singer also shared with the *Chicago Sun-Times* that the band is currently working on a new album, and hinted they'd be doing something special to celebrate the fifteenth anniversary of the 2008 reunion album *The Block*. The official news was announced in September 2023, sharing that *The Block Revisited* was coming out that November.

The newly reworked edition also included previously unreleased bonus material and a two-LP vinyl format for the first time in New Kids' career. Even more special, the album introduced their latest collaborators, K-Pop band SEVENTEEN, who helped helm "Dirty Dancing (Dem Jointz Remix)."

"*The Block Revisited* is a celebration of the magical bond that we've built over the last 15 years," Donnie said in a press release. "*The Block* album didn't only mark the reunion of our band—it sparked the reunion of our band with our fans! I could never over-estimate how much the songs and the spirit, of this album, mean to all of us."

As far as the future, the world is the New Kids' oyster. In the spirit of their ongoing

NKOTB performs during an Atlanta stop on the Mixtape Tour in July 2022.

ABOVE: NKOTB celebrates the release of "Bring Back the Time" with a skate social in New Jersey in 2022.

LEFT: It's an alphabet of musical talent, as NKOTB meets BTS at the 2021 American Music Awards.

The New Kids perform at a Mixtape Tour stop in 2022 in Atlantic City.

collaborations with other boy bands and '80s/'90s contemporaries, there will likely be more mash-ups in the future—and, if they get their way, a full-blown tour with their idols and predecessors New Edition.

"We've been talking about that for years. I think eventually it'll happen," Jonathan told *PopCulture* in 2022. "We did it with the Backstreet Boys, and I never would've thought that we would've done that with them. We did the AMAs, and then we've had BBD (Bell Biv DeVoe) on our shows in the past . . . We were both formed by the same producer, we're from the same neighborhood in Boston, and we've been through a lot of similar experiences, so yeah, it's great. We'll see what happens."

BLOCKHEADS UNITE!
(AT FIRST-EVER CONVENTION)

With the success of the New Kids On The Block annual cruise and their ever-loyal fan base (below), in May 2023 the band tried a new idea "on land" with the first-ever fan convention. Staged in the suburbs of Chicago over Memorial Day weekend, BLOCKCON provided three full days of events, including a concert, prom party, and Q&A panels.

"This year marks the 15-year anniversary of NKOTB reuniting (OMG—can you believe it?). This is not just the anniversary of the band getting back together but it's the anniversary of when our BH Community and mutual love for each other was reborn. We can't let this important milestone pass without a proper celebration! So . . . We are inviting our Blockhead family to come together in Chicago WITH US and take over an entire town for a weekend celebration of all things NKOTB," a message to fans reads on the official BLOCKCON website.

All five members were present for the activities, as Donnie confirmed to the *Chicago Sun-Times*. "Typically, people do conventions, and it's sort of like minimal sightings of the band or the actor . . . but our fans have come to expect a certain level of involvement from us, which means to be there the entire time. There's no event [at BLOCKCON] that doesn't involve us. So it's not going to be like we show up for a half-hour and say hi on a panel or take some pictures and leave. We are full-on there."

He also mentioned that fans were even able to acquire some new ink, if they so desired, to forever pledge allegiance to their favorite band. "So many New Kids fans get tattoos, I wanted to repay them, and I got my own New Kids tattoo in tribute. The artist who did it—so many fans try to seek him out—so he's actually going to come to the convention and do tattoos if anyone wants them."

"We decided let's celebrate all boy bands, throughout the generations ... all the way to the new groups of today, BTS, 1D, you name it."

—Donnie on *Good Morning America* in 2019 to promote "Boys In The Band"

Jonathan, Joey, Jordan, Danny, and Donnie attend the 2021 American Music Awards.

CHAPTER THIRTY-ONE

AN ONGOING LEGACY

New Kids On The Block can't take all the credit for the boy band phenomenon that has continued well into the new millennium. That honor, they would say, goes to New Edition. As Donnie shared in a video introducing the "Battle of Boston" showdown at the 2021 American Music Awards, "Here's all you need to know about New Edition: if there was no New Edition, there would be no New Kids On The Block, no Boyz II Men, no Backstreet Boys, no NYSNC, no O-Town, no One Direction, no LFO, nothing. *Nothing.*"

But it's hard to deny NKOTB's incredible impact on boy bands and pop music in general. They are not only one of the biggest bands of all time, with 80 million albums sold worldwide and one of the highest-grossing tours ever, and a complete study in merchandise marketing. Their influence has also been felt throughout the past five decades. As *Grammy.com* so astutely observed, New Kids On The Block "set the boy band blueprint" for all acts to come. NKOTB was far from the first boy pop group, but they "were the first to set the template that would be applied to every group of all-singing, all-dancing guys who ever adorned the pages of *Tiger Beat*."

Without New Kids On The Block, Lou Pearlman wouldn't have met the act on one of his private planes and decided to start his own enterprises with Backstreet Boys and NSYNC. Without New Kids On The Block as the first to perform the Super Bowl Halftime show, we wouldn't have seen Justin

AND THE AWARD GOES TO . . .

New Kids On The Block's long legacy can also be seen in the awards they've been nominated for and won over the years, from the early days to the 2.0 comeback.

AMERICAN MUSIC AWARDS (below)
- Won Favorite Pop/Rock Band/Duo Group (1990)
- Won Favorite Pop/Rock Album for *Hangin' Tough* (1990)
- Nominated for Favorite Pop/Rock Band/ Duo Group (1991)

BILLBOARD MUSIC AWARDS
- Named No. 1 Pop Artist (1990)

GRAMMY AWARDS
- Nominated for Best Music Video, Long Form for *Hangin' Tough* (1990)

MTV VIDEO MUSIC AWARDS
- Nominated for Best Choreography In A Video (1989)

NICKELODEON KIDS' CHOICE AWARDS
- Won Favorite Male Musician/Group (1990)
- Won Favorite Song for "Hangin' Tough" (1990)
- Nominated for Favorite Song for "Step By Step" (1990)

VIRGIN MEDIA MUSIC AWARDS
- Nominated for Best Comeback (2008)

Timberlake or Lady Gaga do the same. Without New Kids On The Block and their own ventures into reality TV, would Simon Cowell have had the foresight to establish *The X Factor* and give us One Direction?

The band's legacy can even be seen today in the rise of K-pop in the US, where bands like BTS, Tomorrow x Together, Blackpink, New Jeans, and more have dominated the market. According to *NPR,* America is the third-largest importer of K-pop after just Japan and China. One of the country's biggest events, Lollapalooza, has also catered to the market, continuing to book K-pop acts for their annual event. BTS has their own "army" in the States and was the first K-pop band to track on the *Billboard Hot 100* chart and receive Grammy nominations. Yet, "[New Kids'] shoulders are the ones that groups like BTS stand upon," *Entertainment Weekly* affirmed after NKOTB and New Edition's American Music Awards performance in 2021 (to which members of BTS were seen dancing in the crowd).

According to the *New York Theatre Guide*, in a preview of the Broadway musical *KPOP* in 2022, "The rise of MTV in America in the 1990s, and the international success of boy bands such as New Kids On The Block, actually gave way to K-pop idol culture. Korean entertainment moguls wanted to create a similar star system in the Asian market, but it's no wonder K-pop eventually made the jump to the American scene." Much like boy bands of the '80s and '90s, K-pop stars of today are highly choreographed, have incredible business models for merch, and rely on eager fan bases that are all too keen to give themselves nicknames.

In many ways K-pop fills a void left by many of the American boy bands that, unlike NKOTB, abandoned ship in the past 20 years. "We used to have very prominent boy bands and girl groups, such as New Kids on the Block, Spice Girls, One Direction. I think K-pop really hits kind of a vacuum that Western pop cultural trends left behind," UCLA professor Suk-Young Kim told *CBS News.*

The rise of K-pop as a new generation boy band phenomenon is also one that the New Kids fully embrace. Not only did they shout out groups like BTS in their song "Boys In The Band," but Donnie even wore BTS merch to the red carpet at the AMAs in 2021 and was eager to meet the band.

"Having been a member of a boy band that went to the AMAs as a young man, and received screams that never stopped for the duration of the entire show (so much so that other people's fans actually started booing us back—true story), I can tell you that these guys #BTS handled the event with so much grace," he captioned an Instagram photo with the group. "They loved their fans for their support (aka #BTSARMY), they gave love and respect to every single artist they came across, and they never stopped being humble, the entire night. I was proud to wear their T-shirt on the red carpet and am more proud that I did after meeting them."

With New Kids' latest music release offering a collaboration with K-pop band SEVENTEEN, it only hints at the generational overlap that could pave a new way forward for NKOTB to reach even more milestone anniversaries to come. As Donnie once told *WGN News,* "We're bringing back the memories and making new memories at the same time."

THE RIGHT STATS

New Kids On The Block
in New York in 1989.

TIMELINE

1984

New Kids On The Block forms in Boston in producer Maurice Starr's Roxbury studio. ⬇

1986

APRIL 1, 1986: New Kids On The Block's eponymous debut album is released.

1988

APRIL 16, 1988: "Please Don't Go Girl" is released as the first single from upcoming album *Hangin' Tough*.

JULY 19, 1988: New Kids On The Block head out on their first tour with Tiffany. ⬆

AUGUST 12, 1988: NKOTB's sophomore album *Hangin' Tough* is released.

OCTOBER 7, 1988: The New Kids play the Apollo Theatre for the first time, an "Amateur Night" performance of "Please Don't Go Girl" and "You Got It (The Right Stuff)."

1989

APRIL 10, 1989: New single "I'll Be Loving You (Forever)" is released and lands at No. 1 on the *Billboard Hot 100*, the band's very first No. 1 hit.

APRIL 24, 1989: Former Massachusetts governor Michael Dukakis declares New Kids On The Block Day.

AUGUST 22, 1989: *Hangin' Tough*'s final single, "Cover Girl," is released and lands at No. 2 on the *Billboard Hot 100* chart. With its success, NKOTB is the first teen act that enjoyed five Top 10 hits from one album.

SEPTEMBER 19, 1989: NKOTB's holiday album, *Merry, Merry Christmas*, is released. The single "This One's For the Children" hits No. 7 on the *Billboard Hot 100* chart.

END OF 1989: Maurice Starr is named *Billboard's* Songwriter of the Year, in large part due to the hits he churned out for New Kids On The Block that year.

1990

JANUARY 20, 1990: New Kids On The Block appear on the American Music Awards and receive two accolades: Favorite Pop/Rock Duo or Group and Favorite Pop/Rock Album for *Hangin' Tough.*

APRIL 23, 1990: NKOTB wins big at the Nickelodeon Kids' Choice Awards, taking home Favorite Male Musician/Group and Favorite Song for "Hangin' Tough."

MAY 10, 1990: The pre-album single "Step By Step" comes out, selling 1 million copies in its first couple months on record store shelves; it remains the band's biggest song to date.

JUNE 5, 1990: *Step By Step* is released, after fans placed 2 million advance orders.

JUNE 23, 1990: The Magic Summer Tour kicks off in Lake Placid, New York. ↑

NOVEMBER 15, 1990: A new album is released, though this time it's all remixes: *No More Games: The Remix Album.*

DECEMBER 1990: New Kids On The Block is named the No. 1 Pop Group at the inaugural *Billboard* Music Awards.

1991

JANUARY 27, 1991: New Kids On The Block become the first contemporary pop act to perform the Super Bowl Halftime Show.

1992

FEBRUARY 10, 1992: New Kids On The Block appear on *The Arsenio Hall Show* to refute claims of lip-synching and perform live as proof.

1994

JANUARY 25, 1994: After taking a year and a half out of the spotlight (and splitting with long-time producer Maurice Starr), New Kids On The Block released their fifth LP, *Face The Music.*

APRIL 1, 1994: NKOTB hits the road on the Face The Music Tour, playing small, intimate clubs—though without Jonathan.

JUNE 1994: New Kids On The Block officially breaks up.

1996

NOVEMBER 8, 1996: Donnie takes on his first major acting role in the Ron Howard-directed flick, *Ransom*, starring Mel Gibson.

1999

MARCH 16, 1999: Joey releases his debut solo album, *Stay The Same*, produced with his own money and sold on his website.

MAY 25, 1999: Jordan releases his solo debut, *Jordan Knight*, on Interscope, who had originally signed him to the label in 1996.

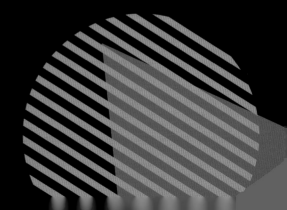

SEPTEMBER 20, 1999: Danny's mom Betty Wood passes away after a battle with breast cancer. Danny begins rallying NKOTB fans to donate toward cancer research.

2001

OCTOBER 16, 2001: Joey takes his first off-Broadway gig, appearing as composer Jonathan Larson in a production of *tick, tick... BOOM!*, kicking off his career onstage as an actor.

2003

JULY 29, 2003: Danny's solo debut, *Second Face*, is released via BMG.

2008

JANUARY 26, 2008: An article on *People.com* announces New Kids On The Block are eyeing a "comeback" (though official word wouldn't come down for two more months).

APRIL 4, 2008: All five members of NKOTB appear on *The Today Show* to officially announce the band is back together after fourteen long years, with the reunion including a new album and tour that year. ⬆

SEPTEMBER 2, 2008: New Kids On The Block's comeback album, *The Block*, is released on Interscope.

SEPTEMBER 18, 2008: The reunion tour New Kids On The Block Live kicks off in Toronto.

2009

MAY 15, 2009: The inaugural NKOTB Cruise sets sail.

2011

JANUARY 29, 2011: Jonathan confirms in a brief post to fans that he is gay.

MAY 24, 2011: The debut album of NKOTBSB (the supergroup of New Kids On The Block and Backstreet Boys) hits the market.

JUNE 11, 2011: NKOTB plays Fenway Park for the first time as part of the NKOTBSB Tour (they'll return two more times, in 2017 and 2021).

2013

JANUARY 28, 2013: A new single is released, an up-tempo R&B soul number called "Remix (I Like The)," NKOTB's first new music in five years.

APRIL 2, 2013: The band's new album, *10*, is released, their tenth record to date (counting compilations and remix albums).

MAY 30, 2013: NKOTB is one of the featured acts at the Boston Strong concert to raise funds for those affected by the Boston Marathon bombings the month prior.

2014

JULY 10, 2014: A four-night mini-residency called "New Kids On The Block: After Dark" begins in Las Vegas at the Axis Theater at Planet Hollywood. ↑

SEPTEMBER 2, 2014: *Nick & Knight* is released, the debut album of the collaborative duo formed by Nick Carter and Jordan Knight. The album enters the *Billboard 200* album chart at No. 24.

OCTOBER 9, 2014: New Kids On The Block get their very own star on the Hollywood Walk Of Fame.

2017

DECEMBER 1, 2017: NKOTB releases a deluxe edition of the *Thankful* EP called *Unwrapped*; it features three new holiday songs, the first time they've released Christmas music since 1989.

2018

OCTOBER 7, 2018: The New Kids return to Apollo Theatre for an emotional show honoring the thirtieth anniversary of both *Hangin' Tough* and the day they first took the stage for the infamous "Amateur Night." →

2020

APRIL 24, 2020: NKOTB releases the "House Party" track and video to cheer people up during the COVID-19 pandemic.

2021

NOVEMBER 21, 2021: New Kids On The Block and New Edition come together at the American Music Awards in the playful "Battle of Boston" showdown.

2022

MARCH 3, 2022: NKOTB's latest single, "Bring Back The Time," is released, a total throwback featuring Mixtape Tour cohorts Salt-N-Pepa, Rick Astley, and En Vogue.

2023

MAY 26, 2023: The first-ever BLOCKCON fan convention is held outside Chicago, providing three full days of events, including a concert, prom party, and Q&A panels.

NOVEMBER 3, 2023: NKOTB celebrates fifteen years of *The Block* with the *Revisited* remix album; most notable is their collaboration with K-pop stars SEVENTEEN.

DISCOGRAPHY

NEW KIDS ON THE BLOCK

Original Release Date: April 1, 1986
Record Label: Columbia Records

Singles:

★ "Be My Girl"
  (March 5, 1986)

★ "Stop It Girl"
  (July 6, 1986)

★ "Didn't I (Blow Your Mind This Time)"
  (August 11, 1989) – the lead single on
  Columbia's re-release effort in 1989

Producers: Maurice Starr, Larkin Arnold, Erik Nuri

Sales: 3 million U.S. (3.3 million worldwide)

Re-released by Columbia in August 1989

HANGIN' TOUGH*

Original Release Date: August 12, 1988
Record Label: Columbia Records

Singles:

★ "Please Don't Go Girl"
  (April 16, 1988)

★ "You Got it (The Right Stuff)"
  (November 7, 1988)

★ "I'll Be Loving You (Forever)"
  (April 10, 1989)

★ "Hangin' Tough"
  (July 3, 1989)

★ "Cover Girl"
  (August 22, 1989)

Producers: Cecil Holmes, Maurice Starr.
Danny Wood, Donnie Wahlberg, Jordan Knight

Sales: 8 million U.S. (16 million worldwide)

*A thirtieth anniversary album was
released on March 8, 2019*

MERRY, MERRY CHRISTMAS

Original Release Date: September 19, 1989
Record Label: Columbia Records

Singles:

★ "This One's For The Children"
  (October 12, 1989)

Producers: Al Lancellotti, Dick Scott,
Donnie Wahlberg, Kenny Nolan, Maurice Starr,
Michael Jonzun, Peter Work, Winston Johnson

Sales: 2 million U.S. (2.3 million worldwide)

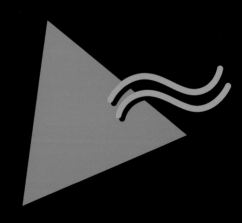

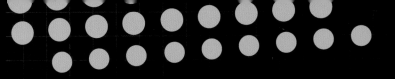

STEP BY STEP

Original Release Date: June 5, 1990

Record Label: Columbia Records

Singles:

★ "Step By Step"
(May 10, 1990)

★ "Valentine Girl"
(June 18, 1990)

★ "Tonight"
(July 26, 1990)

★ "Let's Try It Again"
(September 20, 1990)

Producers: Al Lancellotti, Dick Scott, Leo Okeke, Mark Doyle, Maurice Starr, Michael Jonzun, Richard Mendelson, Taharqa Aleem

Sales: 3 million U.S. (20 million worldwide)

....

NO MORE GAMES: THE REMIX ALBUM

Original Release Date: November 15, 1990

Record Label: Columbia Records

Singles:

★ None

Producers: Remix material largely done by Robert Clivilles and David Cole of C+C Music Factory

Sales: 1.05 million worldwide

....

FACE THE MUSIC

Original Release Date: January 25, 1994

Record Label: Columbia Records

Singles:

★ "If You Go Away"
(December 14, 1991)—
first released on H.I.T.S. greatest hits album

★ "Dirty Dawg"
(December 21, 1993)

★ "Never Let You Go"
(January 11, 1994)

Producers: Brad Young, Donnie Wahlberg, Danny Wood, Jordan Knight, Dow Brain, Jason Hess, Larry Thomas, Leon Sylvers III, Mike Mani, Monty Seward, Narada Michael Walden, Richard Wolf, Walter Afanasieff

Sales: 138,000 U.S.

....

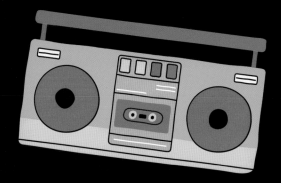

DISCOGRAPHY

THE BLOCK

Original Release Date: September 2, 2008
Record Label: Interscope

Singles:

★ "Summertime"
(May 13, 2008)

★ "Single"
(August 12, 2008)

★ "Dirty Dancing"
(December 19, 2008)

★ "2 In The Morning"
(February 23, 2009)

Producers: Adam Messinger, Adida Kavarro, Akon, Aliaume Thiam, Donnie Wahlberg, Emanuel Kiriakowu, Hakim Abdulsamad, Jimmy Iovine, Martin Kierszenbaum, Nasri Atweh, Ne-Yo, RedOne, Timbaland

Sales: 332,000 U.S.

A fifteenth anniversary edition called The Block Revisited *was released November 3, 2023*

10

Original Release Date: April 2, 2013
Record Label: The Block/Boston Five

Singles:

★ "Remix (I Like The)"
(January 28, 2013)

★ "The Whisper"
(August 1, 2013)

Producers: Brent Paschke, DEEKAY, Gabe Lopez, New Kids On The Block

Sales: 48,000 in its first week

THANKFUL (EP)

Original Release Date: May 12, 2017
Record Label: NKOTB Music

Singles:

★ "One More Night"
(March 7, 2017)

Producers: Brent Paschke, Gabe Lopez, Joe McIntyre, Jussifer, Kelvin Parker, Lars Halvor Jensen, Rob Persaud

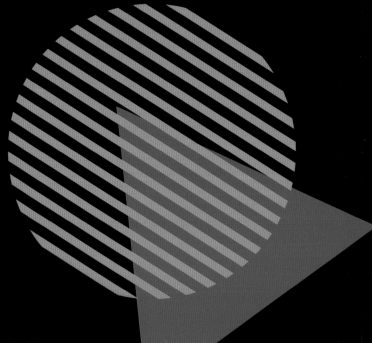

NKOTB onstage
in London in 1991.

ABOUT THE AUTHOR

Selena Fragassi is a fifteen-year music journalist who is currently a regular contributor for the Chicago Sun-Times. Her byline has also appeared in *SPIN, Loudwire, The A.V. Club, Paste, Nylon, Popmatters, Blurt, Under the Radar*, and *Chicago Magazine*, where she was previously on staff as the Pop/Rock Critic. Selena's work has been anthologized in *That Devil Music: Best Music Writing* and she has appeared on televised panels regarding music matters for WTTW's "Chicago Tonight." She is also a member of The Recording Academy.

ACKNOWLEDGMENTS

To my amazing mom, who continues to be my trusted second set of eyes and the first to read my articles (even when I finish them at 4 a.m.); to my supportive father, who always buys out the gas station of newspapers any time I have a story published; to my ride-or-die sidekick brother, who is always my favorite plus-one; and to the memory of our family "Motown Sunday" dance parties that made me realize early on the pure joy and connection music can bring.

SHE'LL BE LOVING HIM FOREVER

It was the third grade, 1990, and Melissa H. promised me her extra ticket to see New Kids On The Block, who were playing the Rosemont Horizon outside Chicago that November. I studied my *Step By Step* VHS tape like I was trying to pass the bar exam. I went through all my neon bike shorts and HyperColor tees to assemble my best outfit. I got the crimper plugged in and ready twenty-one days early. And then, without warning, I was uninvited.

This is my earliest memory of my New Kids On The Block fandom and also my earliest experience with earth-shattering heartbreak. I cried into my NKOTB bedsheets for a week straight. Melissa and I never spoke again. As time went on, just a couple years later, I too had moved over to loving grunge music, like so many other elder Blockheads, though the new object of my affection still fit the bill—the Australian rock boy band, Silverchair. By the eighth grade, someone brought in their old archive *Tiger Beat* magazine from 1991, ripped a page out from the back of the book, and with a gaggle of hyena-laughing classmates, ran over to shove it in my face and press me, "Is this you?" Sure enough, there in black and white was my love letter to Donnie Wahlberg, (right) accompanied by a photo of me in my AYSO soccer uniform, my name and hometown printed below it all. I was mortified. What I didn't know then is that that letter, cringe as it may be (I really do blame it on sleeping on those bedsheets night after night), would become my first piece of music writing, more or less. It has since morphed into a fifteen-year career that has taken me to incredible highs, interviewing and reviewing some of the artists I have also come to love over time, whether it was getting to know Adele for one of her first American profiles to spending a day with Jack White in Nashville for a cover story. This book, my first, is truly a full-circle moment, a new love letter to New Kids On The Block, who in no small way continue to inspire a generation.

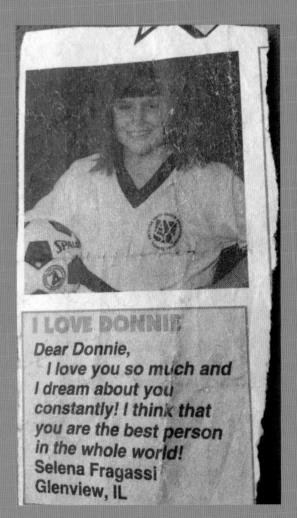

I LOVE DONNIE

Dear Donnie,
    I love you so much and I dream about you constantly! I think that you are the best person in the whole world!
Selena Fragassi
Glenview, IL

IMAGE CREDITS

Getty Images. **Page 143** Steve Granitz/WireImage/Getty Images. **Page 144** Callahan/ Everett Collection/Alamy Stock Photo. **Page 145** Larry Marano/Getty Images Entertainment. **Page 146-147** James Devaney/WireImage/Getty Images. **Page 148** Matt Stone/MediaNews Group/Boston Herald/Getty Images. **Page 150** L. Busacca/ WireImage/Getty Images. **Page 152** Axelle/Bauer-Griffin/FilmMagic/Getty Images. **Page 153** Robin Platzer/Images Press/Getty Images. **Page 154** Angela Rowlings/ Media News Group/Boston Herald/Getty Images. **Page 155** Barry King/WireImage/ Getty Images. **Page 156** John Bohn/The Boston Globe/Getty Images. **Page 158** Bruce Glikas/Film Magic/Getty Images. **Page 159** Walter McBride/Getty Images Entertainment. **Page 160** Al Pereira/Michael Ochs Archives/Getty Images. **Page 161** Rick Madonik/Toronto Star/Getty Images. **Page 162** Jose Perez/Bauer-Griffin/GC Images/Getty Images. **Page 164** Moviestore Collection Ltd/Alamy Stock Photo. **Page 165 Above Left** Photo by George Pimentel/WireImage/Getty Images. **Page 165 Above Right** Steve Granitz /WireImage/Getty Images **Page 165 Below** MediaNews Group/ Boston Herald/Getty Images. **Page 166** Universal Images Group North America LLC/ Alamy Stock Photo. **Page 167** TCD/Prod.DB/Alamy Stock Photo. **Page 168** Michael Bush/UPI/Alamy Stock Photo. **Page 171** Paul Zimmerman/WireImage/Getty Images. **Page 172** Amanda Edwards/Stringer/Getty Images Entertainment. **Page 173** L. Busacca/WireImage/Getty Images. **Page 174** FOX/Getty Images. **Page 175** David L. Ryan/The Boston Globe/Getty Images. **Page 176** Jamie McCarthy/WireImageGetty images. **Page 178** Michael Loccisano/FilmMagic/Getty Images. **Page 181** George Napolitano/FilmMagicGetty Images. **Page 182** Faith Ninivaggi/Media News Group/ Boston Herald/Getty Images. **Page 184-185** Joe Corrigan/Stringer/Getty Images. **Page 186-187** Kevin Winter/AMA2010/Getty Images Entertainment. **Page 188** Vallery Jean/Film Magic/Getty Images. **Page 190** John Parra/WireImage/Getty Images. **Page 192 Above** Alexander Tamargo/Getty Images Entertainment. **Page 192 Below** Alexander Tamargo/Getty Images Entertainment. **Page 193** John Parra/ WireImageGetty Images. **Page 194** Janette Pellegrini/WireImage/Getty Images. **Page 196** Ron Galella, Ltd./Getty Images. **Page 197** Paul Marotta/Stringer/Getty Images Entertainment. **Page 198** George Pimentel/WireImage/Getty Images. **Page 200** Theo Wargo/WireImage/Getty Images. **Page 201** Matthew J. Lee/The Boston Globe/Getty Images. **Page 202** Matthew J. Lee/The Boston Globe/Getty Images. **Page 203** Jon Super/Redferns/Getty Images. **Page 204-205** Bobby Bank/WireImage/Getty Images. **Page 206** Janette Pellegrini/WireImage/Getty Images. **Page 208** Kevin Winter/ AMA2010/Getty Images Entertainment. **Page 210** Paul Marotta/Stringer/Getty Images Entertainment. **Page 211** Stephen M. Dowell/Orlando Sentinel/Tribune News Service/Getty Images. **Page 213** Michael Tran/FilmMagics/Getty Images. **Page 214-215** Noam Galai/Getty Images Entertainment. **Page 216** Becker/WireImage/ Getty Images. **Page 218-219** Amanda Edwards/WireImage/Getty Images. **Page 221** Andrew Chin/Getty Images Entertainment. **Page 222** Miikka Skaffari/Film Magic/ Getty Images. **Page 224-225** Taylor Hill/Film Magic/Getty Images. **Page 227** Angela Rowlings/MediaNews Group/Boston Herald/Getty Images. **Page 228** Tim Mosenfelder/Getty Images/Entertainment. **Page 230** Paras Griffin/Getty Images Entertainment. **Page 231 Above** Manny Carabel/Getty Images Entertainment. **Page 231 Below** Matt Winkelmeyer/Getty Images Entertainment. **Page 232** Donald Kravitz/ Getty Images Entertainment. **Page 233 Left** WENN Rights Ltd/Alamy Stock Photo. **Page 233 Right** Robyn Beck/AFP/Getty Images. **Page 234** Axelle/Bauer-Griffin/ FilmMagic/Getty Images. **Page 236** Ron Galella, Ltd/Ron Galella Collection/Getty Images. **Page 238-239** Bette Marshall/Contour/Getty Images. **Page 240 Left** John R. Nordell/Archive Photos/Getty Images. **Page 240 Right** Ron Galella, Ltd/Ron Galella Collection/Getty Images. **Page 241** Steve Castillo/San Francisco Chronicle/Hearst Newspapers/Getty Images. **Page 242** Jamie McCarthy/WireImage/Getty Images. **Page 243 Above** Ethan Miller/Getty Images Entertainment. **Page 243 Below** Noam Galai/Getty Images Entertainment. **Page 247** Pete Still/Redfern/Getty Images.

INDEX

First published in 2024 by Epic Ink, an imprint of The Quarto Group,
142 West 36th Street, 4th Floor, New York, NY 10018, USA
(212) 779-4972 • www.Quarto.com

Epic Ink titles are also available at discount for retail, wholesale, promotional, and bulk purchase. For details, contact the Special Sales Manager by email at specialsales@quarto.com or by mail at The Quarto Group, Attn: Special Sales Manager, 100 Cummings Center Suite 265D, Beverly, MA 01915 USA.

10 9 8 7 6 5 4 3 2 1

ISBN: 978-0-7603-8985-0

Digital edition published in 2024
eISBN: 978-0-7603-8986-7

Library of Congress Control Number: 2023949626

Group Publisher: Rage Kindelsperger
Editorial Director: Lori Burke
Creative Director: Laura Drew
Managing Editor: Cara Donaldson
Editor: Katie McGuire
Text: Selena Fragassi
Interior Design: Kegley Design
Cover Design: B. Middleworth and Kegley Design

Printed in China

NEW KIDS ON THE BLOCK · STOP IT GIRL · DIDN'T I (BLOW YOUR MIND) · POPSICLE · ANGEL · BE MY GIRL · NEW KIDS ON THE BLOCK · ARE YOU DOWN · I WANNA BE LOVED BY YOU · DON'T GIVE UP ON ME · TREAT ME RIGHT · HANGIN' TOUGH · YOU GOT IT (THE RIGHT STUFF) · PLEASE DON'T GO GIRL · I'LL BE LOVING YOU (FOREVER) · COVER GIRL · I NEED YOU · HANGIN' TOUGH · I REMEMBER WHEN · WHAT'CHA GONNA DO (ABOUT IT) · MY FAVORITE GIRL · HOLD ON · MERRY, MERRY CHRISTMAS · THIS ONE'S FOR THE CHILDREN · LAST NIGHT I SAW SANTA CLAUS · I'LL BE MISSING YOU COME CHRISTMAS (A LETTER TO SANTA) · I STILL BELIEVE IN SANTA CLAUS · MERRY, MERRY CHRISTMAS · THE CHRISTMAS SONG · FUNKY, FUNKY XMAS · WHITE CHRISTMAS · THE LITTLE DRUMMER BOY · THIS ONE'S FOR THE CHILDREN · STEP BY STEP · TONIGHT · BABY, I BELIEVE IN YOU · CALL IT WHAT YOU WANT · LET'S TRY IT AGAIN · HAPPY BIRTHDAY · GAMES · TIME IS ON OUR SIDE · WHERE DO I GO FROM HERE? · STAY WITH ME BABY · FUNNY FEELING · NEVER GONNA FALL IN LOVE AGAIN · FACE THE MUSIC · YOU GOT THE FLAVOR · DIRTY DAWG · GIRLS · IF YOU GO AWAY · KEEP ON SMILIN' · NEVER LET YOU GO · KEEPIN' MY FINGERS CROSSED · MRS. RIGHT · SING · YOU WALKED INTO MY LIFE · LET'S PLAY HOUSE · I CAN'T BELIEVE IT'S OVER · I'LL STILL BE LOVING YOU · I'LL BE WAITIN' · THE BLOCK · CLICK CLICK CLICK · SINGLE · BIG GIRL NOW · SUMMERTIME · 2 IN THE MORNING · GROWN MAN · DIRTY DANCING · SEXIFY MY LOVE · TWISTED · FULL SERVICE · LIGHTS, CAMERA, ACTION · PUT IT ON MY TAB · STARE AT YOU · 10 · WE OWN TONIGHT · REMIX (I LIKE THE) · TAKE MY BREATH AWAY · WASTED ON YOU · FIGHTIN' GRAVITY · MISS YOU MORE · THE WHISPER · JEALOUS (BLUE) · CRASH · BACK TO LIFE · NOW OR NEVER · SURVIVE YOU · LET'S GO OUT WITH A BANG